The Insurance Spectator Of London...

Anonymous

[REGISTERED FOR] [TRANSMISSION ABROAD.

THE INSURANCE SPECTATOR OF LONDON

London: Published at The MODERN PRESS, 14, Paternoster Row, E.C.
[ENTERED AT STATIONERS' HALL.] [PUBLISHED SEMI-MONTHLY.

Vol VI., No. 58   JANUARY 1, 1884.   Price 4d.

POSITIVE GOVERNMENT SECURITY
LIFE ASSURANCE COMPANY, LIMITED.

HEAD OFFICE:—

34, CANNON STREET,
LONDON, E.C.

MANAGER AND ACTUARY:

G. MACKENZIE,
F.F.A., A.I.A.

Those about to
ASSURE are requested
to examine the System of
The **POSITIVE**, which is unlike
any other and is **UNEQUALLED** for
SIMPLICITY, SECURITY, AND LIBERALITY.

The POSITIVE is the ONLY Company in which the Assured can stop
payment at any time without a sacrifice.

The POSITIVE is the ONLY Company the Bankruptcy of which would
affect its Policyholders.

Prudential Assurance Company,

LIMITED,

HOLBORN BARS, LONDON.

THIRTY-FIFTH ANNUAL REPORT.

For the Year ending 31st December, 1883.

THE DIRECTORS have much pleasure in presenting their Report and Accounts for the year 1883.

The reduction in the rate of Expenditure in both branches has been continued during the year.

The Funds of the Company have been increased during the year by the sum of £759,818, in the Ordinary Branch £126,255, and in the Industrial Branch £633,563, raising the total assets of the Company to £3.807,217.

It will be seen that the Investments of the year have been confined to the usual first-class securities.

ORDINARY BRANCH.

The New Business of this Branch for the year consists of 9,504 Policies, assuring the sum of £1,166,392 and producing a New Annual Premium Income of £46,959.

The claims of the year amount to £86,075, representing 526 Deaths and 21 Endowment Assurances matured.

The Annual Premium Income at the end of the year is £200,790, being an increase of £35,841 over the year 1882. The increase for 1882 was £22,216, making a total increase in the Premium Income for the first two years of the Quinquennium of £58,057.

The rate of Expenditure of the Branch slightly exceeds ten per cent. on the Premium Income.

INDUSTRIAL BRANCH.

The Premiums actually received during the year in this Branch are £2,504.307 14s. 2d. as compared with the sum of £2,126,022 3s. 11d. received during 1882, being an increase of Premium Receipts of £378.285 10s. 3d. The increase for 1882 was £276,527 5s. 6d., making a total increase in the Premium Receipts for the first two years of the Quinquennium of £654,812 15s. 9d.

The Claims of the year amount to £912,333.

The total expenses of this Branch, as compared with those of the previous year, show a reduction in the rate of expenditure of Two and a half per cent. on the Premium Income.

The Directors have thought it advisable to make a further addition to their number, and they have invited Dr. ROBERT BARNES, of Harley Street, one of the original Shareholders of the Company, to a seat at the Board. Dr. BARNES's election will be submitted to the Meeting for confirmation.

The vacancy in the Auditorship has been filled by the appointment of Mr. THOMAS WHARRIE, of Glasgow, a duly qualified Shareholder.

Save, pinch, scrimp, if you must, but lay by *something* to take the place of your labor when the work of your hands for those you love shall have ceased for ever.

------◆------

A story is told of a citizen of Memphis who recently died, who had put away two policies of insurance on his life so very carefully that no one could find them until a friend of deceased had a dream in which he saw the policies in an out-of-the-way drawer. On getting up in the morning he was so impressed with the dream that he went to the place dreamed about and found them.

------◆------

Mark Twain says that he has been looking into the matter of accident and life insurance. Last year he travelled 20,000 miles by rail; the year before he travelled over 25,000 miles, half by sea and half by rail; and the year before somewhere about 10,000 miles, exclusively by rail. He things that 60,000 miles in three years is about what he travelled. And never an accident, and in the same time nearly 50,000 out of New York's 1,000,000 of people died in their beds. " That is appalling," he says, " the danger isn't in travelling by rail, but in trusting to those deadly beds. I will never sleep in a bed again." And now his advice to all people is " don't stay home any more than you can help; but when you have got to stay home a while buy a package of these insurance tickets and sit up nights. You cannot be too cautious."

------◆------

Clothes on Fire: What to Do.—Three persons out of four would rush right up to the burning individual and begin to paw with their hands without any definite aim. It is useless to tell the victim to do this or that, or call for water. In fact it is generally best not to say a word but to seize a blanket or any other fabric—if none is at hand, take any woollen material—hold the corners as far apart as you can, stretch them out higher than your head, and running boldly to the person, make a motion of clasping in the arms, mostly about the shoulders. This instantly smothers the fire and saves the face. The next instant immerse the burnt part in cold water, and all pain will cease with the rapidity of lightning. Next apply some flour; if possible put the patient in bed, and do all that is possible to soothe until the physician arrives. Let the flour remain until it falls off itself, when a beautiful new skin can be found. Unless the burns are deep, no other applications are needed. The dry flour for burns is the most admirable remedy ever proposed, and the information ought to be imparted to all. The principle of this action is that, like the water, it causes instant and perfect relief from pain by totally excluding the air from the injured parts.

Professor Huxley calls for a hanging day among careless builders as the most effective means of checking the erection of badly built and tumble down houses. This is a prime joke, but fire insurance companies will second the professor in carrying it to its logical conclusion.

------◆------

When any one dies they ask in France: " How old was he?" In Germany, " What complaint did he die of?" In America they say: " A good thing he is dead at last!" In Italy: " Poor fellow!" In Russia: " He doesn't need to work any more; he is well off!" In Holland they ask: " How much money has he left?" and in England: " Was he insured?"

------◆------

Bulwer's Resolution.—Early one morning Bulwer, the novelist, returned to his hotel, from a gambling house, where he had been passing the last hours of the night. For the first time in his life he had played high; and, with the insidious good fortune so frequently attendant on the first steps along what would otherwise be the shortest and least attractive pathway to perdition, he had gained largely. The day was dawning when he reached his own rooms. His writing desk stood upon a *console* in front of a mirror; and pausing over it to look up his winnings, he was startled and shocked by the reflection of his face in the glass behind it. The expression of the countenance was not only haggard, it was sinister. He had risked far more than he could afford to lose; his luck had been extraordinary, and his gains were great. But the ignoble emotions of the night had left their lingering traces in his face; and as he caught sight of his own features still working and gleaming with the fever of vicious excitement, he, for the first time, despised himself. It was then he formed the resolution that, be the circumstances of his future life what they might, no inducement, whether of need or greed, should again tempt him to become a gambler.

------◆------

" Old Letters."

" It seems but yesterday she died, but years
Have passed since then; the wondrous change
    of time
Makes great things little, little things sublime,
And sanctifies the dew of daily tears.
She died, as all must die; no trace appears
In History's page, nor save in my poor rhyme,
Of her, whose life was love; whose lovely
    prime,
Passed sadly where no sorrows are, nor fears,
It seems but yesterday; to-day I read
A few short letters in her own dear hand,
And doubted if t'were true. Their tender grace
Seems radiant with her life! Oh! can the dead
Thus in their letters live? I tied the band,
And kissed her name as though I kissed her
    face,"

PERSONALS.

Mr. D. M. Conner to be London secretary of the *Scottish Imperial.* Mr. Conner was formerly chief clerk in the London office.

Mr. R. D. Alliger of New York, United States manager of the *Imperial* Fire Insurance Company, is on his annual visit to the Southern States.

Mr. Stephenson Bell, of Sunderland, formerly with the *Western Counties* Office, has been appointed District Superintendent for the *British Empire Mutual* Life Office.

Mr. R. F. Russell, the able and learned editor of the *Finance Chronicle,* has gone to Italy to recruit his health, followed, we are sure, by the good wishes of his many friends.

Mr. W. H. Wills, M.P., at an extraordinary general meeting of the *British Empire Mutual* Life Assurance Society, was elected director in the place of the late Mr. Benham, deputy-chairman.

Mr. Willard Welch, for many years associated with the insurance agency of Welch, Ten Eyck and Lansing at Albany, N.Y., has been appointed special agent for the State of New York for the *City of London* Fire Insurance Company to succeed Special Agent Parsons, resigned.

Edward James Gray, Esq., Alderman.—It is announced that Edward James Gray, Esq., Alderman, of the firm of Anderson, Fairley, and Gray, Colonial Brokers, Mincing Lane, London, has joined the London Board of the *London and Lancashire* Fire Insurance Company.

Mr. F. J. Lee-Smith, late Managing Director of the *Globe* Plate Glass Insurance Company, Limited, and more recently Managing Director to the *Globe* General Insurance Company, Limited, is now Managing Director of the *Universal* Plate Glass Insurance Company, Limited.

Mr. J. M. DeCamp of Cincinnati, the general agent of the *Liverpool and London and Globe,* was surprised by the presentation at his office of an elegant marble clock and obelisk ornaments of Egyptian design, the gift of some forty managers and agents in Ohio in appreciation of his past services as president of the Ohio State Board, to which position he has been recently re-elected.

OBITUARY.

On the 9th inst., Mr. Jas. White, of Overtoun, Glasgow, died at his residence, in Dumbartonshire. Besides being a director of the *City of Glasgow* Life Office, he was chairman of the Glasgow Royal Exchange, and the City of Glasgow Bank Relief Fund, the Daphne Fund, and many public institutions. He was one of the wealthiest men in Glasgow.

On the 29th ult., Mr. James Richard Lloyd died at his residence, Shrubbery Cottage, Lee, Kent. For 14 years he represented the Lewisham and Plumstead Board of Works at the Metropolitan Board. Only nine days before his death Mr. Lloyd was re-elected a director of the *Provident Clerks'* Life Office, a position he had held for no less than 13 years.

Mr. Samuel Bowly, the great temperance advocate, and a Director of the *United Kingdom* Temperance and General Provident Institution, has, at a ripe old age, passed over to the majority.

MULTUM IN PARVO.

☞ **PROVINCIAL HAIL.**—The Provincial Hail Insurance Company (Limited) is to be wound up voluntarily Messrs. E. Snelling and A. L. Lewis, F.C.A., have been appointed liquidators.

☞ **LAW REVERSIONARY.**—At the thirty-first annual general meeting of the Law Reversionary Interest Society (Limited), the reports of the Directors and Auditors were adopted, and a dividend at the rate of £6 per cent. per annum, free of income tax, was declared.

☞ **SCEPTRE LIFE ASSOCIATION.**—Dividend, at the rate of six per cent. per annum, and a bonus of £1 per share. During the past year 932 policies were issued assuring £172,550, and producing in annual premiums £4,982. The claims amounted to £13,085 with bonus additions.

☞ **SCOTTISH TEMPERANCE.**—The report for six months of the Scottish Temperance Life Assurance Company shows that 297 life policies for £59,425 were completed, yielding a premium income of £2,290. For accidents 189 policies for £77,800 were issued, yielding in premiums £271

☞ **CYCLISTS'.**—The Cyclists' Accident Assurance Corporation (Limited), announce an issue of unsubscribed capital. The company was formed a few months since, and the prospectus states that the growth of the business is already sufficient to justify the expectation of a prosperous future.

☞ **SCOTTISH PROVIDENT INSTITUTION.** —The new business of the past year was 1,694 proposals for £1,041,923, with premiums £37.885; £28,868 further was received for annuities. The claims were £199,109, with £30,620 of bonus additions. The realised funds at 31st December, 1883, amounted to £4,736,292, showing an increase of £333,383.

☞ **FIRE INSURANCE ASSOCIATION.**—The report of the Fire Insurance Association (Limited) for last year states that the net premiums, after deducting £54,350 for re-insurances, amounted to £244,129, and the losses to £180,542. The balance carried forward to the credit of next year's account amounts to £20,373, and the total funds stand at £270,373.

☞ **LAW UNION.**—At the meeting of the Law Union Fire and Life Insurance Company the report stated that the new insurances for the year in the fire department amounted to £6,527,789, yielding in new premiums £8,626, and that in the life department 266 new policies had been issued, insuring £216,157, the new premiums upon which amounted to £7,373. Dividend ; 3s. per share, being equal to 25 per cent.

☞ **LEGAL AND GENERAL.**—At the annual general meeting of the Legal and General Life Assurance Society it was stated that the new premiums received in the past year amounted to £10,037, and the sums assured to £290,000, The total income was £222,000, exclusive of £3,998 profits on investment realised. After providing for all outstanding claims, the funds of the society amounted to £2,042,651.

☞ **EAGLE INSURANCE COMPANY.**—At the meeting it was stated that the premiums received in respect of assurances completed during the past year amounted to £19,379, assuring £472,430. Of the above-mentioned total of £472,430, the sum of £172,000, has been re-assured, at premiums amounting to £6,698, of which £4,379 represents single premiums, effecting assurances for £69,500. The claims amounted to £381,115.

☞ MUTUAL FIRE.—The report of the Mutual Fire Insurance Corporation (Limited), shows that the net premiums amounted to £217,547 19s. 9d. The losses of the the year reached £133,528 5s. 5d., and the balance to the credit of revenue account is £21,247 10s. 7d. The reserve fund stands as before at £136,951 2s., and interest thereon at the rate of 5 per cent per annum, amounting to £6,847 11s. 1d. was paid to the members in December last.

☞ LONDON GUARANTEE and ACCIDENT. —At the meeting of the London Guarantee and Accident Company (Limited) the directors reported that the new premiums for 1883 were £13,451 5s. 2d. The total income for the year was £40,158, 8s. 8d., and the claims £25,740. A dividend of 5 per cent. free of income tax, was declared. The reserve fund amounts to £35,000, and the assets of the company at Dec. 31st were £96,491 10s. 9d.

☞ LONDON, EDINBURGH, and GLASGOW. —At the meeting of the London, Edinburgh, and Glasgow Assurance Company (Limited), the report was adopted. It showed the premium income for that year to be 3·6 per cent. over the income of 1882. In the accident department a bonus of 12½ per cent. to policy-holders of three years' standing was declared, with an extra bonus of 7½ per cent., making 20 per cent. in all, to total abstainers. A dividend of 5 per cent. for 1883 was declared,

☞ LONDON AND LANCASHIRE.—The report of the London and Lancashire Life Assurance Company for 1883 states that the new assurances amounted to £544,890, under 1,591 policies, giving a new premium income of £18,357. The net premium income for the year amounted to £102,853, and after payment of all outgoings, including cash bonuses to policy-holders and dividend to shareholders at the rate of 15 per cent., the sum of £32,302 was added to the funds, which now stand at £332,628.

☞ LONDON AND PROVINCIAL.—From the report of the London and Provincial Fire Insurance Company (Limited) for the year 1883 it appears that the premiums, after providing for re-insurances, amounted to £187,773, and the losses paid and outstanding to £130,791. Following precedent, the directors have written off to current revenue the sum of £4,159, being one-fourth of the amount paid for preliminary and organisation expenses to Dec. 31, 1882. The balance carried forward is £7,688.

☞ NATIONAL LIFE ASSURANCE.—According to the report of the National Life Assurance Society the premium income of 1883 was £74,314 4s. 7d., and the Revenue account showed a total, including the funds at the beginning of the year, of £959,695 1s. 5d. The claims were heavier than usual, and the Assurance Fund at the end of the year exhibited a reduction of £15,633, the amount being £828,225 19s, 1d. The total, however, is still £31,054 higher than it was at the end of 1881. The invested funds were yielding interest at the rate of £4 14s. 9d. per cent, per annum.

☞ EQUITY AND LAW.—At the annual meeting of the Equity and Law Life Assurance Society the report stated that the business for the past year amounted to £522,082, under 232 policies, of which £347,955 had been retained by the society. The amount of new premiums was £11,695 8s. 7d. The total assurances in force at the end of the year was £4,525,311 10s., the premiums on which amounted to £131,634 1s. 10d. The society's assets now amount to £1,871,757 6s. 1d., having been increased by the sum of £53,326 0s. 5d., being the difference between the receipts and payments during the year.

☞ LONDON ASSURANCE CORPORATION. —At the general court of the London Assurance Corporation, the recommendation of the Court of Directors that the dividend for the half-year ending at Lady Day, 1884, should be 35s. per share, free of income-tax, was adopted. The governor, in announcing this recommendation, stated his expectation that the dividend in October next would be the

usual amount of 15s. per share, which would make 20 per cent. for the year on the paid up capital. At the same court Mr. Charles George Arbuthnot (of the firm of Messrs. Arbuthnot, Latham, and Co.) was elected a director of the corporation.

☞ UNITED KINGDOM BOAT and FISHER- MEN'S.—Notice has been given that an Extraordinary General Meeting of the United Kingdom Boat and Fishermen's Accident Insurance Company (Limited), would be held at the offices of the Company, No. 7, Union Court, Old Broad Street, yesterday, for the purpose of considering and, if thought fit, passing a resolution that the Company be wound up voluntarily, under the provisions of the Companies' Acts, 1862 and 1867, and that Ernest Albert Harrison-Ainsworth, of 107, Cannon Street, London, Public Accountant, be appointed Liquidator, for the purposes of such winding-up.

☞ NORTH BRITISH and MERCANTILE.— At a meeting to-day of the general court of directors of the North British and Mercantile Insurance Company it was reported that, including £60,475 brought forward, the balance at the credit of profit and loss of the fire department was £223,303 15s. 4d., out of which it was resolved to recommend that a dividend of 20s. per share should be paid, together with a bonus of 10s. per share—one half of the dividend, along with the bonus, being paid on the 5th prox., and the balance on Oct. 6th. It was further resolved to recommend that £25,423 0s. 1d. should be carried from profit and loss to reserve, thereby increasing that fund to £1,170,000, and that the balance of £52,986 15s. 3d. at the credit of profit and loss should be carried forward.

IMPERIAL UNION ACCIDENT ASSURANCE COMPANY LIMITED.

REPORT.

In presenting the accompanying Report and Accounts for 1883 the Directors desire to offer the Shareholders their congratulations on the marked progress which has been made by the Company since their last Report.

The New Policies of the year numbered 3,253 and produced premiums to the amount of £8,845 10s. 8d., against 2,144 policies yielding £5,399 1s. 1d. in the previous year.

The entire premium income was £26,256 16s. 7d. as compared with £21,020 1s. 9d. in 1882.

The number of Claims paid upon General and Railway Policies was 915 and amounted to £12,733 13s. 11d. Amongst them were four claims for Fatal Accidents amounting to £2,480.

A small but remunerative business has been transacted during the year in the Employers' Liability Branch, which it is the Directors' intention to encourage and develope.

The excess of the Revenue over the Expenditure of the year is £3,293 17s. 3d., out of which the Board have allotted £1,080 to increase the claim reserve, £300 has been written off the value of the lease, and £159 2s. 1d. appropriated to increase the reserve for deductions from Agents' Balances, whilst £26 13s. 0d. has been written off Furniture account, leaving a net balance of Profit of £1,728 2s. 2d. Out of this the Directors recommend that a dividend of 5 per cent. be paid, which will absorb £1,031 19s. 0d., leaving £696 3s. 2d. to be carried forward to next account.

The Directors who retire by rotation are Messrs. W. Goulding, and R. P. Edwards, and they being eligible, offer themselves for re-election.

The Auditors, Messrs. George N. Read and John H. Tilly also retire, and offer themselves for re-election.

W. H. GOULDING,
Secretary.

The sum paid for Life Insurance should not be regarded as an *expense*, but as an *investment*, like a deposit in bank, to meet a contingency ever liable to occur, when otherwise want and misery may take the place of comfort and happiness in the family circle,

WESLEYAN AND GENERAL ASSURANCE SOCIETY.

QUINQUENNIAL VALUATION.

The forty-third annual meeting of this association was held at the Grand Hotel, Colmore Row. Mr. Benjamin Smith presided, and the directors present were Messrs. J. Field, C. Edgerton, D. Barr, J. Manley, N. Brecknell, J. Hunt, J. Marriott, J. A. Mountford, J. J. Poole, C. Osborn, C. Rowe, J. Simons, and J. Smith, R. A. Hunt (general manager), J. W. Lewis (deputy manager), &c.

The directors' report stated that the auditors have examined the securities and accounts, and have certified to their correctness. The total number of members at December 31st, after allowing for deaths, lapses, and surrenders, was 165,212, being an increase of 48,194 as compared with the previous year. The total income from all sources amounted to £94,215 5s. 10d. The amount paid for claims, including sick-pay, medical attendance, bonuses, and surrenders was £47,079 14s. 1½d., making a total of £590,481 12s. 1½d. paid for claims since the society was established. The funds at the end of the year stood at £177,937 0s. 1d., against £170,909 5s. 6d. as compared with the previous year. Fifteen new districts have been opened out during the year, and 705 new agents appointed. This has necessary entailed considerable expenditure, but, as the result, the premium income has been increased during the year by £13,069, as compared with an increase of £3,015 in the year 1882. The amount advanced on mortgages is less by £6,696 than last year, this being occasioned by the repayment of several large sums on mortgage at the end of the year, too late to be reinvested before the close of the year. The past year concluded the term of five years from the last quinquennial valuation, and in accordance with the rules of the society, the directors instructed Mr. H. W. Manly, of London, to make a valuation of the assets and liabilities of the life department, as at December 31st, 1883; and the report would be submitted to the members at the close of the present meeting. The retiring directors were Messrs. C. Rowe, J. Smith, and J. While. Mr. While, in consequence of failing health, did not seek re-election.

The Chairman, in moving the adoption of the report, congratulated the members on the continued progress of the society. The report recorded the largest increase in the number of members and premium income that had been reported in any year since the establishment of the society, Encouraged by the success which attended the opening of new districts in the year 1882, the directors continued the extension of the society's operations, the result being the success he had mentioned. A satisfactory feature in the year's transactions would be found in the fact that while there had been a rapid increase of business, the claims had not abnormally increased, the ratio of claims to premium income bearing favourable comparison with previous years. The question might be asked why, with an augmented income and a normal death-rate, the balance on the year was smaller than that obtained as the result on the transactions of 1882, and the answer was that a rapid extension such as that reported meant a large increase under the head of extension expenses. the whole of the business procured being paid for within the year in which it was obtained, but the result might be looked for with confidence in the current year. Reference had been made in the report to the valuation of the Life Branch, and while he did not wish to anticipate the actuary's report, he could not refrain from referring to the subject for the purpose of expressing the satisfaction of the directors that, notwithstanding the fact that the annual meeting was held two months earlier than in previous years, it had been possible to supply the actuary with the necessary data for making the valuation sufficiently early to enable him to report the result to the meeting.

Mr. J. Field, in seconding the proposition, spoke of the gratifying progress that had been made by the society during the past year, and expressed his belief in the continuance of its prosperity.

The report was adopted.—On the motion of Mr. Woodward, seconded by Mr. Whitworth, a vote of thanks was accorded to the Board of Directors for the able and efficient manner in which they had discharged their duties.—Mr. J.

Smith responded.—The voting upon the electing of directors then took place by ballot, Mr. G. While being elected in the place of Mr. J. While, who retired.

A special meeting was then held to receive the report of Mr. H. W. Manly, the actuary. The following is the report:—"The valuation of the life department of your society having been submitted to me, I have much pleasure in stating that the figures show the department to be in a satisfactory condition. At the last valuation there were 55,501 policies in force, insuring £847,681, and there are now 160,530, insuring £1,941,084, showing a marked development in the business of the society during the quinquennium. This has necessarily entailed a great increase in the labour required in the preparation of the details for valuation and the subsequent calculations. From my acquaintance with the general character of the work, I am satisfied that every care has been taken to insure accuracy, and great credit is due to your manager, Mr. Hunt, and his assistants for the rapid and admirable manner in which the work has been executed. The figures show the net liability of the society to be £86,579, and as the total funds amount to £97,424, there is consequently a surplus of £10,845. including the undivided surplus on the last occasion. This will provide a bonus of 1 per cent. per annum on the sums assured on all participating policies which have been two years in force.—Signed, H. W. Manly, actuary."

The Chairman said the bonus which the Board recommended to be declared was at the same rate as on the last occasion, and, considering the rapid extension of the society during the last five years, entailing, as it did, increased expenditure in consequence of the business having to be paid for, must be considered a very satisfactory one. The Board had every confidence that the future would be even more prosperous than the past, and would no doubt result in larger profits being divided. Notification of the respective amounts allotted to each participating policy-holder would be forwarded as early as possible, as soon as the necessary certificates were made out. The Chairman then moved the adoption of the actuary's report.

Mr. J. Manley, seconded the motion, and it was carried.—On the proposition of the Chairman, seconded by Mr. David Barr, it was resolved, " That a bonus of £1 per cent. per annum for the past five years upon the sum assured be declared and distributed amongst the participating policy-holders who have paid two or more annual premiums out of the surplus of £10,845 as reported by Mr. H. W. Manly upon the life assurance endowment and annuity departments of the society at December 31st, 1883."—A vote thanks to the Chairman concluded the proceedings.

LONDON, EDINBURGH & GLASGOW ASSURANCE COMPANY.

ANNUAL REPORT, 1883.

The Directors beg to submit the Report on the operations of the Company during the year 1883, together with the Revenue Accounts and Balance Sheet to 31st December last, made up in accordance with the Life Assurance Companies' Acts, and the Company's Articles of Association.

As was intimated to the Shareholders in September last, the Directors have entered upon Industrial Life business, that is, the assurance of small sums by weekly and monthly premiums. Before doing so they had given the matter prolonged consideration, and they willingly embraced an opportunity of commencing this business, under very favourable circumstances, which was offered by the retirement of an Industrial Company, and they are glad to report that the results to the 31st December, 1883, fully justify the step thus taken. After five months trial, estimates prepared by the Manager of the results to be obtained by a moderate expenditure were carefully considered by the Directors, and it was decided, at the commencement of the current year, to act on the recommendations of the Manager, and to largely extend the operations of this Branch. The Shareholders will, doubtless, regard the undertaking of Industrial Business as an event of great importance. The Directors have the Manager's assurance, and believe with him, that, up to the present time, the results have been thoroughly satisfactory, and that this description of business will prove a source of strength and profit to the Company. Whilst the Directors will continue to act cautiously, they are convinced that an energetic policy, controlled by effective supervision, is essential to the success of Industrial business, and upon these principles their operations will be conducted.

During the year 1883, 488 proposals for the Assurance of £114,330 were received in the Ordinary Life Department, of which 50 proposals for £8,279 were declined, and 342 Policies were issued, assuring £64,592, the annual premium income thereon (excluding the additions made for Accident risks under Combined Life and Accident Policies) being £2,159 1s. The remaining proposals were either not proceeded with or were in course of completion at the close of the year. In the Industrial Branch, under the circumstances above stated, 7,707 Policies, assuring £104,186 10s., were issued during five months the premiums payable thereon being £4,072 13s. 2d. per annum. In the Accident Department the number of Policies issued was 710, insuring £455,650, the new premium income (including the additions made for Accident risks under Combined Life and Accident Policies) being £2,045 14s. 11d. It will thus be seen that the total annual premium income on the new business of the year was £8,277 9s. 1d., which the Directors consider satisfactory, especially when it is borne in mind that the attention of the executive, during five months of the year, was very largely occupied in organising the Industrial Branch.

The accompanying accounts show the financial position of the Company. It will be observed that the total premium income for the year, after deducting reassurances was £10,800 15s. 4d., which, as against a total premium income of £7,926 0s. 11d. during the previous twelve months, shews an increase of 36 per cent. The Life Assurance Fund has been increased from £15,900 5s. 8d. to £17,090 6s. 6d., and the Accident Insurance and Reserve Funds from £6,784 13s. 3d. to £7,565 17s. 1d. The increase in these funds represents the total "net premiums" for the year, after deducting Claims and Policies, Surrenders, Annuities, and Bonus to Policyholders, accumulated at 4 per cent. interest, and maintains those funds at the respective amounts required by the Articles of Association.

In view of the state of the Accident Insurance Account, the Directors have resolved to allow to Policyholders who had paid three years' premium previously to 31st December last, a bonus of 12½ per cent. on the current year's premium, irrespective of any compensation which may have been paid to them; also to allow, upon the same conditions, the extra bonus of 7½ per cent., making 20 per cent. in all, to Total Abstainers.

From the Balance Sheet it will be observed that the British and Colonial Government Securities alone exceed the Life Assurance and the Accident Insurance and Reserve Funds

The Average rate of interest on the investments was £4 4s. 9d. per cent. on the 31st December, 1883.

With regard to the payment of interest, the Directors, notwithstanding their report of the 19th February, 1883, deemed it advisable to delay any payment pending the question of the establishment of the Industrial Department, which might have required an outlay larger than would have been consistent with such payment. They have now, after careful consideration, decided to recommend payment of interest on the paid up capital of the Company, in pursuance of the powers conferred by Article 86, at the rate of £5 per cent. for the past year.

The Directors have to report that Mr. William Blewitt has been elected a Director of the Company, to fill the vacancy caused by Mr. Ashhurst's death. In accordance with the Articles, Mr. William Blewitt, Sir John Humphreys, Mr. Samuel Rowles Pattison and Mr. Edward Leigh Pemberton, M.P., retire from office on the present occasion, but, being eligible, offer themselves for re-election, and are recommended accordingly. The Auditors, Messrs. Broom, Hays & Akers, and Mr. John Templeton also retire, but are eligible for re-election.

Signed on behalf of the Board of Directors,

E. LEIGH PEMBERTON, Chairman.

WILFRED A. BOWSER, Manager and Actuary.

C. WEEDING SKINNER, Secretary.

33, New Bridge Street, E.C.

London, 3rd March, 1884.

LAW INTELLIGENCE.

(Sitting at Nisi Prius, before MR. JUSTICE GROVE *and a Special Jury.)*

NEWTON V. THE POSITIVE GOVERNMENT SECURITY LIFE ASSURANCE COMPANY (LIMITED).

Mr. M'Intyre, Q.C., and Mr. E. Gill were counsel for the plaintiff; Mr. Waddy, Q.C., and Mr. Purcell appeared for the defendants.

This was an action to recover damages for a malicious prosecution. The plaintiff, who is now a commercial traveller to a firm of distillers, has been in the tea trade and the business of a wine merchant in Little Trinity Lane. About July, 1882, when he was still a wine merchant, he had as clerk and traveller a Mr. Meaden, and this gentleman had a daughter who was engaged to a young gentleman named Gavegan. For the benefit of this latter, and as the defendant's witnesses swore, with a view to teach him the wine business in the plaintiff's house, the defendant society advanced on August 1, 1882, the sum of £400. This was paid by cheque, less deductions, to Meaden for £346 15s., and he endorsed it to the plaintiff, who paid it into his private banking account, adding some more to make up a sum of £350. In his private ledger this appeared as £347. As security the defendants required a promissory note for £400, which the plaintiff signed, payable on September 14, 1883, when Gavegan came of age, and would be entitled to between £2,000 and £3,000 Consols under a will. Gavegan was further to insure his life for £1,000 as security in case of death before majority or bankruptcy. In May, 1883, the plaintiff went into liquidation, and his trustee said his estate might yield 6d. or 9d., or possibly 1s. in the pound. After September 14th the defendants looked in vain for the payment of their £400. They proceeded against Meaden and got judgment against him, and took steps to have him made a bankrupt. Meaden said he was not a partner and penniless. On applying to Gavegan, he said it was "hard lines" he should be called on to pay a large sum of money of which he had had only between £20 and £30. The plaintiff had filed his petition, and said he had handed the money over to Meaden and Gavegan. Under these circumstances the defendant's manager, Mr. Mackenzie, and their accountant, Mr. Turner, consulted their solicitor, and a conference took place with counsel, who advised an information against the three alleged conspirators for unlawfully attempting to defraud. This came on for hearing on summons at the Mansion-house on October 25, 1883, and was adjourned on November 2, 12, and 16, when Alderman Nottage dismissed the charge, the prosecuting counsel admitting there was no case against the plaintiff. This writ was then issued on November 26, and the plaintiff claimed as damages the expenses of his defence, £46 12s. 8d., and personal expenses and loss of custom, £11 4s. The plaintiff's account was that he had paid Meaden £110 in cash, but that Meaden on striking a balance was still in his debt, and he had paid him more than the £346 15s. His counsel put the case to the jury as one where the criminal law was put in force as a screw to "squeeze" payment of the £400 out of the plaintiff. The case for the defence was that they had acted without malice, and with reasonable and probable cause for the course they took. While making no imputation on the plaintiff's honesty now, they said he must suffer for having got into such dishonest company, and much reliance was placed on the fact that neither Meaden nor Gavegan were called as witnesses.

Mr. Justice Grove summed up, and said the questions for the jury would be whether the defendants had acted maliciously and without reasonable or probable cause. If so, then the plaintiff was entitled to such reasonable damages as they might award. Now "malice" did not mean personal spite or animosity, but any improper or sinister motive such as reasonable men would not be actuated by, and which ought not to actuate a man in bringing a misdemeanant to justice. It was for the Judge to say whether there was an absence of reasonable and probable cause, which was an evidence of malice, on the facts found by the jury, and that sometimes became embarrassing as to the number of such questions to be put and the deductions to be drawn from any grouping of the answers. Did the defendants make proper inquiries by their agents as to the plaintiff, so as to justify a fair and discreet person in acting as they did? Were the answers they got reasonably sufficient to induce them to institute the prosecution? And so did they act *bond fide* and without malice? If they acted for the purpose of "squeezing" money out of the plaintiff that would be in law malice, for no man had a right to use the criminal law for that purpose. As to the loss of reputation, the character of a man after liquidation did not stand so high as that of a perfectly sound and solvent man. But he could not lay down any sum or rule as to that. As to the loss of custom the evidence before them as to that was slender, but the plaintiff was entitled to recover his necessary expenses. They would not award him vindictive damages, but reasonable and proper compensation as they thought him deserving of if he was entitled to a verdict.

The jury retired, and after an absence of 20 minutes, returned into Court with a verdict for the plaintiff —damages £150.

THE MUTUAL FIRE INSURANCE CORPORATION LIMITED.

REPORT OF THE COMMITTEE OF MANAGEMENT.

To the Fourteenth Annual General Meeting of the Members of the Mutual Fire Insurance Corporation, Limited, held in the "A" Committee Room, Old Town Hall, Manchester, on Wednesday, the 26th March, 1884.

The Directors have pleasure in submitting to the Members the following Report and Statement of the affairs of the Corporation for the year ending the 31st December last.

The balance to the credit of the Revenue Account is £21,247 10s. 7d., mainly derived from Foreign sources. This business, the profit on which belongs to the members, has necessitated the customary heavy payments on account of Commission, etc., but it is anticipated that the maximum ratio of expense to premiums, that of the average of leading Companies, has been reached.

The accounts and securities have been examined by two independent auditors, whose certificate is annexed.

During the year £20,627 0s. 6d. was deducted from premiums on account of discounts and allowances. Since the formation of the Corporation in 1870 insurers have benefited to the amount of £201,366 16s. 8d. under these heads.

James Priestley, Esq., of Huddersfield, has been appointed a Director in the place of the late H. Dyson Taylor, Esq.

The Members of the Committee of Management retiring by rotation and eligible for re-election are, Thomas Brooke, Esq., Huddersfield; Edward Charrington, Esq., London; Samuel Cooke, Esq., Liversedge; Charles J. Galloway, Esq., Manchester; James Priestley, Esq., Huddersfield; and William Taylor, Esq., Oldham.

The Auditors, Messrs. J. C. Stead and Edwin Guthrie, retire, but offer themselves for re-election.

The Reserve Fund now stands at £136,951 2s.; and Interest thereon, at the rate of 5 per cent. per annum, amounting to £6,847 11s. 1d., was paid to the Members in December last.

By Order of the Committee of Management,
THOMAS BROOKE, *Chairman.*
Manchester, *March 5th,* 1884.

MR. G. A. REID, secretary of the *Standard* Fire Office, has joined the staff of the *Fire* Insurance Association.

THE ACTUARY, No. 33.

MR. CHARLES RICHARD FISHER,
Actuary of *Economic* Life since 1869.

Mr. Fisher was trained to the business of Life Insurance under Mr. Rainbow, late Actuary of the *Crown*, which office he entered in 1840 as special assistant to the Actuary, and remained there a period of 29 years, becoming its Assistant Actuary. On his retirement he received a handsome testimonial of plate. Mr. Fisher is a member of the Actuaries' Club.—*Insurance Cyclopædia.*

REVIEW.

Mr. Bourne's "Handy Assurance Guide."

We have great pleasure in drawing attention to the announcement, in another column, concerning the April issue of this invaluable and unerring Guide. Other things being equal, the Agent who carries the Guide will do vastly more business than the Agent who tries to do without it.

Useless Criticism.—Of all unprofitable and irritating uses of the tongue, the most useless and the least profitable, within the range of the not immoral and vicious, is its use in criticism of things done, that are not to be done over again, and cannot be helped. To cry over spilled milk is bad enough: to scold over it is still worse; even though the scolding be of a very mild type. This Spectator being of the male gender, is inclined to think that such criticism is a somewhat feminine habit. "My dear," says the minister's wife just as her husband is going into the pulpit, "what an awful spot you have got on your coat!" The poor man cannot take it off then; and the only effect of the irritating and useless bit of knowledge is to make him painfully conscious of a spot that probably no one else in the congregation perceives but himself and his wife. She had better "put a guard on her lips," and take the spot out quietly when the parson gets home. "I have cut out a couple of trees so as to give us a good view of the valley, and let in a little more sun and air." "Oh, dear! what did you do that for? I am so sorry to lose those trees." It is always the special tree that *he* has cut down that *she* is so sorry to lose. But after the mischief is done it neither makes him nor her feel any happier to go into mourning about it. It is a good rule, with rare exceptions, never to criticise a thing that is done unless it be for the special purpose of securing something better for the future.

THE ATTENTION OF PERSONS effecting LIFE ASSURANCES is directed to the terms offered by the SCOTTISH METROPOLITAN LIFE ASSURANCE COMPANY. The Premiums are fully 20 per Cent. lower than usual, while the Conditions of Assurance are extremely liberal, and the Security is unusually complete. Full particulars on application to the Secretary, at the Head Office, 25, St. Andrew's Square, Edinburgh, or at the London Office, 79, Cornhill, E. C.

LONDON AND NORTH WESTERN FIRE
INSURANCE COMPANY, LIMITED.

HEAD OFFICE :—MANCHESTER.

Applications for Agencies to be addressed to

SAMUEL BUTLER, MANAGER.

SUN LIFE OFFICE,

63, THREADNEEDLE STREET, LONDON, E.C.
Established 1810.
Low PREMIUMS.   LARGE BONUSES.
Guaranteed Security.   Immediate Settlements.
TONTINE BONUS SCHEME.
(See Prospectus, which may be had on application.)
BONUS DECLARED, £1,536,035.

Now Ready. Demy 8vo. Price One Shilling.
SURRENDER VALUES, with Tables of Minimum Surrender Values, as at ages 20, 30, and 40.
Demy 8vo.   Price One Shilling,
HOW TO POPULARISE LIFE ASSURANCE.—
Addressed to Agents.
Reprinted from the FINANCE CHRONICLE.
London : RUSSELL & CO., 8, John Street, Adelphi, W.C.

L'ETERNELLE

INSURANCE COMPANY, LIMITED.
Head Office—1, Place Boieldieu, PARIS.
Head Office for Great Britain—4, Broad Street Buildings,
Liverpool Street, London, E.C.
Manchester Branch , ... 75, Princess Street.
Glasgow Branch . . . . . 134½, West George St.
Capital - - - - - £200,000.

This Company is prepared to entertain proposals on special and other risks. Agents wanted. Liberal terms.

INTEGRITY ASSURANCE SOCIETY.

Established 1858.
ENROLLED BY ACT OF PARLIAMENT.

Chief Offices:

30 & 28, WELLINGTON STREET, STRAND,
LONDON, W.C.
Industrial Life and Endowment Assurances effected.
District Managers of Life, Fire, and Accident offices are invited to apply for District Agencies. Terms, Liberal Commission and Bonuses

JOHN T. HARRIS,
General Manager.
JOHN P. NASH Secretary.

"To Life Agents no more thoroughly useful publication is offered."

THE HANDY ASSURANCE GUIDE.

The April issue is now ready, containing the latest Reports of all offices to date.
The Liverpool Mercury says :—" Possesses all the comprehensiveness of details and correctness of analysis which have made it valuable as well as handy. It contains a variety of information of an exceedingly useful character."
PRICE 3d. 2s. 6d. PER DOZEN.

W. BOURNE,
79, BELMONT DRIVE, NEWSHAM PARK,
LIVERPOOL.

LION FIRE INSURANCE COMPANY, LIMITED

JAMES S. FORBES, ESQ., Chairman.
FIRE INSURANCES on Liberal Terms. Losses promptl y
settled.
Head Office ;—5, LOTHBURY, LONDON, E.C.
Applications invited for Agencies in Unrepresented districts

ADVERTISEMENTS.

Outside Cover	£10	10
Inside ,,	7	7
,, Page	6	6
,, Half Page	3	15
,, Quarter Page	2	0

N. B.—Advertisers are requested to make their Post-Office Orders payable to Mr. W. J. WEST, at the Chief Office, the letters to him being addressed to 5, Ludgate Circus Buildings.

TERMS OF SUBSCRIPTION.

ANNUAL Subscription (including postage), Paid in advance, 9s.

NOTICE TO CORRESPONDENTS.

All Communications intended for insertion to be addressed to the Editor, " The INSURANCE SPECTATOR OF LONDON," 5, Ludgate Circus Buildings, E.C.

ANSWERS TO CORRESPONDENTS.

J. B. H.—Have nothing to do with it.
DELTA,—You should apply to the Secretary of the Institute of Actuaries.
Can any of our Manchester subscribers tell us anything of a concern called the *Oak* Insurance Company, Limited, of 75, Bridge Street, Manchester, and of which a Mr. S. E. Gibbons is Manager and Secretary ?

CONTENTS:

THE
Insurance Spectator of London.

APRIL 1; 1884.

The Home business, and a selected portion of the Continental Insurances, of the *Standard* Fire Office, Limited, has been transferred to the *Fire* Insurance Association, Limited.

The Report of the *Scottish Temperance* Life Assurance Company, for six months, is very satisfactory. Nearly three hundred Life Policies were issued insuring close upon seventy-thousand pounds. In the Accident Department not far short of two hundred policies were taken up for seventy-seven thousand eight hundred pounds. The Company is doing well and may already be pronounced, " A genuine success."

The Eleventh Annual Report of the *Equitable* Fire Insurance Company is before us. The abnormal loss ratio of 1883 has not spared the *Equitable* any more than other high class Fire Offices. After the storm, however, the Assets stood at over a Hundred Thousand Pounds, and the Reserves at nearly Twenty-five Thousand Pounds. The Dividend for the year, moreover, reaches the substantial figure of Ten per cent. The truth is the *Equitable* is managed with so much skill, and directed by gentlemen of such rare business ability, that a bad year only serves to bring out the strong points of the Company. The Accounts are Audited by the leading firm of Accountants in Manchester, Messrs. Halliday, Peon, and Co.

A reference to page 112 will give our readers information concerning the remarkable progress made—during the few months of its existence—by the *Cyclists'* Accident Assurance Corporation. It will also be seen that the unissued portion of the capital may now be applied for. The scheme of the *Cyclists'* is unique, the Directorate strong and influential, and the Executive exceptionally skilled. As an evidence of activity upon the part of the management it is announced that six hundred agents and representatives have already been appointed and Branches founded, on favourable bases, in Liverpool, Glasgow, and Dublin. We have no hesitation in recommending the shares as a most desirable investment, and we advise early application for the same.

The Premium Income of the *Accident* Insurance Company now exceeds fifty-three thousand pounds per annum, and the assets are close upon sixty thousand pounds. At the Annual Meeting held yesterday the Chairman was able to congratulate the Shareholders upon the financial condition of the Company, and the figures more than justified the language he used. The Bonus Allowances to Policy-Holders have increased to upwards of three thousand pounds, while the investments remain at an increased value above the figures at which they stand in the balance sheet. The Company has removed to excellent premises in the very centre of the City, viz:—St. Swithin's House, No. 10, St. Swithin's Lane, and the outlook was never better either for Share or Policyholders, and that means very high commendation.

The fourteenth annual report of the *Mutual* Fire Insurance Corporation, presented on the 26th ult., is a satisfactory record of business carried on during a period of unexampled severity. The statement, signed by Mr. Chairman Brooke, will be found on page 107. The system of the *Mutual* is unique, the members receiving all the profits made by the corporation. Since the *Mutual* was founded—only fourteen years since—upwards of two hundred thousand pounds has been returned to insurers for allowances for Fire extinguishing appliances and discounts. Without doubt this explains the high character of the property insured as well as the growth and popularity of the company. The assets of the corporation, solid and convertible, exceed one hundred and fifty thousand pounds. We congratulate the directors and Mr. Lane upon the high position to which the corporation has attained.

On Thursday the *London and Lancashire* Life Assurance Company will celebrate the attainment of its majority by the holding of its 21st Annual Meeting. The history of the Institution is one of steady growth, uninterrupted by any adverse event whatever. If it be true that " The nation is happy which has no history," it is certainly a fact that the Life Office which can refer to twenty-one years of successful growth, unmarked by a single drawback, is in a very enviable position. Let us glance for an instant at the figures representing the standing of this Company now that it has attained manhood—Premium Income over £111,000 ; Life Funds £332,628 6s. 6d. The Shareholders are to have a Dividend and Bonus at the rate of 15 per cent. We congratulate the *London and Lancashire* upon the attainment of such a splendid position, simultaneously with the 21st year of its existence.

The Directors of *The Fire* Insurance Association have the courage of their convictions. The fourth Annual Report to be presented on Thursday sets forth that after provision for all outstanding losses, expenses, commissions, State and other taxes at home and abroad, there remains a balance at credit of the Company of £20,373 14s. 8d., exclusive of the Reserve Fund of £50,000. The Directors propose to carry this amount forward to 1884, and therefore do not recommend any Dividend. Without doubt the action of the Board will commend itself to the Insuring public, and will do more than anything else to sustain the favour in which the Association is held both in this country and the United States. After all, it is highly probable that it only means waiting one year, for one cannot conceive of another year so disastrous all round for the Fire Offices as the one just closed. The Shareholders in the *Fire* Association have done remarkably well, especially when the youth of the Association is borne in mind, and they may rest assured that *they are in safe and good hands.* With a total security exceeding a million sterling, and an income of upwards of three hundred thousand pounds secured since the year, the Company enters upon its fifth year with everything in its favour, and surpassed for strength and solidity.

The third annual general meeting of the *London, Edinburgh and Glasgow* Assurance Company, was held at the City Terminus Hotel, Cannon Street, on the 12th ult., and the report presented appears on page 105. The directors have acted wisely in entering upon the industrial branch of life insurance and few men are so well fitted as Mr. Bowser to conduct business of this nature. The beginning of the operations is very auspicious and augurs well for the future. According to the chairman of the *Prudential*—an excellent authority—"there appears to be no limit to the amount of business capable of being done in this branch." What the industrial class wants is a thoroughly sound institution, honorably conducted, and paying its claims promptly, all this and more they will have in the *London, Edinburgh and Glasgow.* In the year which has just closed, the premium income shews an increase of 36 per cent., the life funds have risen from £15,900 5s. 8d. to £17,090 6s. 6d., and the accident funds from £6,784 13s. 3d. to £7,565 17s. 1d. The assets of the company now exceed seventy-four thousand pounds. A bonus of 12½ per cent. to accident insurers of three years standing has been declared, and an extra bonus of 7½ per cent., making 20 per cent. in all, to total abstainers. If every agent of the *London, Edinburgh and Glasgow* will at once bend to his work with re-doubled energy, the history of the company for 1884 will be one of large and genuine success.

THE FOREIGN COMPANIES' PROFITS.

The last New York report, says the *Insurance World*, of Pittsburgh, U.S.A., contains some statistics regarding the foreign companies doing business in this country which has not heretofore been made public. It is the amount of money which the home office has sent to the United States during their operations here, and the amount of money which the home office in turn has received from its American branch. The appended table is, however, not quite complete, as the *Imperial* had not reported.

	Remitted to the U. S.	Received from the U. S.
City of London	Dols. 636,855.50	Dols. 85,459.40
Commercial Union	2,165,640.00	1,585,270.00
Fire Insurance Ass'n	302,967.40	....
Guardian	450,000.00	225,089.85
Hamburg Bremen	335,681.53	352,355.26
Imperial	....	....
Lancashire	1,322,412.34	1,908,805.57
Lion	546,275.00	12,985.00
L. & L. & G.	5,797,748.33	10,118,969.16
London & Lancashire	995,840.85	209,495.17
London & Provincial	532,132.81	49,141.19
London Assurance	392,840.00	304,669.09
N. B. & M.	5,633,600.48	4,549,092.40
North German	270,354.93	19,542.89
Northern	252,012.40	162,330.85
Norwich Union	650,471.87	96,536.00
Phœnix	418,235.00	....
Queen	1,014,835.00	968,875.00
Royal	4,447,883 18	4,724,608.40
Scottish Union	709,959.54	....
Sun	847,625.00	45,140.00
Transatlantic	458,501.69	....
United Re-Ins	456,649.81	48,454.00
Total	Dols. 26,668,198.66	Dols. 25,466,819.23

It will be seen that these companies have remitted to the United States 3,201,279.43 dols. more than they have received. But on the first day of January the above named companies (Imperial not included) were possessed of assets in the United

States to the amount of 31,409,650.67 dols.' from which, however, deducting their liabilities, we find that the net assets or surplus was 13,752,715.53 dols., and again from this the balance still due to the home office, and we find that the entire net gains of all the foreign companies in the United States has been 10,551,436.10 dols. Of course, some of this profit is due to interest. Considering the length of time which some of these companies have been here, it is apparent that upon the whole the foreign companies have not drained us of our gold very extensively, as not only has their profit been invested in this country, but over three millions besides. The principal exception is the L. & L. & G., which has absorbed nearly seven millions of this profit.

AT A LONDON FIRE.

Luke Sharp in the Detroit *Free Press* gives this account of his observations at a London fire:

One day I sat on a 'bus top that was wending its way around the rear end of St. Paul's Cathedral into Cheapside. Just as we turned down towards the Bank the driver of a westward 'bus shouted to our driver:

"You'll 'ave to 'urry, Bill, to get through; there's a fire."

Bill hurried, but it was too late. A policeman caught the heads of his horses and he had to go round by the great building of the general post-office. This meant loss of time and perhaps the loss of a trip, and the driver muttered bad English as he turned his horses about. I slipped down from the 'bus and hurried along Cheapside with the crowd, for the police had not yet arrived in sufficient numbers to keep back the populace. At last we came to a tall, narrow building, from the top of which smoke was issuing. The shop keepers on the other side of the way were putting up their shutters, both to keep out possible heat and the crush of a London crowd. The excited throng hustled to and fro, the only cool men being Gog and Magog, who adorned the front of Sir John Bennett's clock store only a few doors nearer the Bank than the fire. I went up a stairway opposite the burning building, came into an up-stairs tailor shop and begged permission to look out on the crowd and at the fire.

The whole street was black with people except a little space in front of us, which the constantly augmented body of police were sturdily trying to widen. Clerks were carrying out piles of ledgers and account books, and everybody was shouting what should be done, but still no firemen appeared. A man in the third story threw up a window and looked down wonderingly on the crowd, gazing now up the street and then down. He evidently was at a loss to know what all this fuss and stoppage of traffic was about. Suddenly he looked aloft, and seeing the smoke shouted: "Oh my gracious," slammed down the window and disappeared. There was a laugh at this.

It reminded me of the old story of the darkey who smelt some one's foot burning, and then suddenly discovered that it was his own.

The smoke now rolled in dense volumes from the upper story, the police managed to close a large space on the street, but still there were no signs of the fire department. Even the crowd began to think they were rather slow, and some one suggested that some one ought to go and tell Capt. Shaw of the fire.

Next the smoke began to ooze from the windows next story from the top. One of the upper panes cracked with the heat, but stayed in its place. I thought I could hear the roar of the flames, but I might have been mistaken. It seemed a criminal waste of time on the part of the fire companies. At last the cry arose, "Here she comes!" Around the statute of Mr. Pitt— I think it is Pitt—at the west end of Cheapside came the tall, red, shaky arms of a fire escape. This was run up against the building and a brass helmeted fireman walked rapidly up the ladder with a hatchet strapped to his belt. Why he didn't go up the stairway, I don't know, except, perhaps, that he felt the department owed something to the crowd for their long waiting, and so he held them breathless while he climbed the spidery arrangement. He looked in at one of the windows, took out his hatchet, put it back again and nodded to the men below. He seemed convinced that there really was a fire. Then he came down again.

A long trail of dark smoke appeared down towards the Bank, and over the dark crowd we could see a brass funnel rapidly approaching. The crowd split as it came, and closed up behind it. The men, all in brass helmets, very speedily got their engine in working order, and a man went up the stairway with a noozle and hose attachment. By this time another engine was in position from the post-office end of the street, and then another. They came silently, for although in John Gilpin's time,

"The stones did rattle underneath
As if Cheapside were mad."

the street is quieter now in the smoothest of asphalte pavement. Presently black water in streams began to pour down the stairway, which opened directly from the street, and after a while the smoke became less dense.

When the fire was almost out a red wagon dashed furiously up, and out of it stepped a man on whose head shone a silver helmet. This was Capt. Shaw. As he passed into the building each fireman raised his open hand up to the side of his helmet in a sort of military salute to the chief. It seemed rather absurd to have men at a fire stop for that sort of disciplinary mummery. However, Capt. Shaw thinks American firemen are lacking in discipline. I think that if it were not for the great stability of London buildings Capt. Shaw would have to trade off some of his English discipline for American briskness in getting to a fire.

PLATE GLASS INSURANCE COMPANIES,

[REGISTERED FOR]   [TRANSMISSION ABROAD.

London : Published at 5, Ludgate Circus Buildings, E.C.

[ENTERED AT STATIONERS' HALL.]   [PUBLISHED SEMI-MONTHLY.

Vol. VI., No. 65.   APRIL 15th, 1884.   Price 4d

The Gresham Life Assurance Society.

ST. MILDRED'S HOUSE, POULTRY, LONDON, E.C.

Assets (1883) - - - - - -	£3,351,200
Life Assurance and Annuity Funds - - -	£3,265,000
Annual Income - - - - - -	£664,094

BRANCH OFFICES.

ENGLAND.

BIRMINGHAM—18, Bennett's Hill.
BRADFORD—Bank Chambers, Bank Street.
BRIGHTON—4, Pavilion Buildings.
BRISTOL—1, Broad Quay.
HULL—Trinity House Lane.

LIVERPOOL—Gresham Buildings, 99, Dale Street.
MANCHESTER—2, Cooper Street.
NEWCASTLE—Percy Buildings, Grainger St. West.
NORWICH—Bank Plain.
SUNDERLAND—37, Fawcett Street.

WALES.

CARDIFF—Gresham House, Roath.

SCOTLAND.

GLASGOW—116, St. Vincent Street.
DUNDEE—74, Commercial Street.

EDINBURGH—97, George Street.
ABERDEEN—28, Market Street.

IRELAND.

DUBLIN—5, Northumberland Street.

MODERATE RATES OF PREMIUM.   LIBERAL SCALE OF ANNUITIES.

Loans granted upon Security of Freehold, Copyhold, and Leasehold Property, Life Interests, and reversions. Also to
Corporate and other Public Bodies upon Security of Rates, &c.

Prospectus, Reports and Proposal Forms can be obtained on application to the Society's Agents and Branch Offices, or to

JOSEPH ALLEN, Secretary

MY TABLETS—MEET IT IS, I SET IT DOWN—*Hamlet.*

No 65.—Vol. VI.　　　APRIL 15, 1884.　　　SEMI-MONTHLY 4d.

SCRAPS.

IN CHURCH—DURING THE LITANY.

I'M glad we got here early, Nell;
　We're not obliged to sit to-day
Besides those horrid Smith girls—well
　I'm glad they go so soon away.
How does this cushion match my dress?
　I think it looks quite charmingly.
"Bowed sweetly to the Smiths?" Oh! yes—
[*Responds*]—" Pride, vanity, hypocrisy,
　　　　　Good Lord deliver us."

I hate those haughty Courtenays!
　I'm sure they needn't feel so fine,
Above us all—for mamma says
　Their dresses aren't as nice as mine,
And one's engaged; so just for fun,
　To make her jealous—try to win
Her lover—show her how 'tis done—
[*Responds*]—" From hatred, envy, mischief, sin,
　　　　　Good Lord deliver us."

To-day the rector is to preach
　In aid of missionary work:
He'll say he hopes and trusts that each
　Will nobly give, nor duty shirk.
I *hate* to give, but then one *must*,
　You know we have a forward seat;
People can see—they *will*, I trust—
[*Responds*]—" From want of charity, deceit,
　　　　　Good Lord, deliver us.

Did you know that Mr. Gray has gone?
　That handsome Mr. Rogers, too?
Dear me! We shall be quite forlorn
　If all the men leave—and *so* few!
I trust that we with Cupid's darts
　May capture some—let them beware—
[*Responds*]—" Beholds the sorrows of our hearts,
　　　　And, Lord, with mercy hear our prayer."

During a strike in Lancashire the mob was threatening and increasing, and the local volunteers were called out. At a crisis in the affair one of the citizen-soldiers levelled his musket at a prominent opponent, when the man next to him struck up the gun, exclaiming, " Don't shoot that man —his life's insured in our office!"

" Gentlemen," said the professor to his medical students assembled in clinic, " I have often pointed out to you the remarkable tendency to consumption of those who play upon wind instruments. In this case now before us we have a well-marked development of lung disease, and I was not surprised to find, on questioning the patient, that he is a member of a brass band. Now, sir," continued the professor, addressing the consumptive, " will you please tell the gentlemen what instrument you play?" " I plays der drum," said the sick man.

Many a man has saved his property to his family by life insurance.

A woman should not scream at the sight of a mouse. It lets the ferocious animal know right where she is located, after which it may advance with the certainty of death upon its quivering prey.

Accidentals.

Unseen Dangers.

In prayer-books generally may be found a note-worthy form of expressing thanks for "mercies known and unknown," and for preservation from "dangers seen and unseen." Unknown blessings received and unseen perils escaped no doubt fill up a large part of our lives. Some of them we fail to recognise through lack of observation, and many pass unnoticed because in the nature of the case we could not at the time detect them. This element of unseen danger weighs very heavily in the estimate of personal risk as applied to accident insurance.

A minister once said that there are two classes of troubles which one should never worry about, those he can help, and those he can't help. So there are two sorts of liability to accident which every man should provide against, the risks he can foresee, and those which he cannot. The former he may sometimes be able to avoid, unless they lie in the direct line of his duty; the latter he can make no calculation about, for he knows neither where or what they are. But he can by means of accident insurance in a good degree compensate the loss of time and money which they inflict.

People in multitudes are going to and fro continually, amid chances of accident of which they are seldom conscious, for most of them are in the category of the "unseen." To be stirred with a harassing sense of the risk they run would for the most part be of no use in avoiding the danger or lessening the risk. It is far better to go our several lawful ways, and using such means for protection as are provided for us. And there is no better earthly provision known than an accident policy.

We hear of many narrow escapes of persons insured, and they deserve consideration as well as the frequent claims for injuries and the large amounts paid to sufferers. Among recent instances is an incident which might have proved a terrible accident, on the steam yacht ———, at the ———. She was crowded with pleasure-seekers, most of whom had no thought of danger. But her engineer was called away that day, and a man supposed to be competent took his place. He let the water get so low that a portion of the boiler became red-hot, and then actually tried to force in cold water. Fortunately there was some hitch in the operation, the captain discovered the cause and drew the fires. Had the cold water entered the boiler the boat would have been blown to atoms. Two gentlemen from ———, having policies to the tune of £1,600, were sitting on deck directly over the boiler. This was a case of danger known after it had passed, but many as great a peril is run by those who never know it. Let every one be thankful for unseen escapes as well as deliverance from obvious dangers. Igno-rance and carelessness are fruitful of possible mischief to innocent persons, and one of the plain conclusions of this brief discourse is that every one should do his part in guarding against the consequences by insuring.

A Home for His Mother.—Among the payments made recently was one of £500 on a freight brakesman in ———, who was run over by the train and soon died. He was the only son of his mother, and she was a widow. Her husband died last year, and left nothing for her support. She told the agent that when her son insured she blamed him for spending the money so foolishly. The day he was hurt and dying, she said to him, "What can I do without you, James?" He replied, "Well, there is my insurance; it will help you." "I would have been almost destitute if I had not this," she says. Now no monument of granite or marble could speak to her of her lost boy as does her comfortable home secured to her by his thoughtful investment in a policy of accident insurance.

A Hero who believed in the Old Moral.—Captain ———, of the steamer—— lost in the terrible storm on November 16th, is the latest proof that a man with a soul as heroic as a viking's may be a prudent and sensible man to boot. The steamer broke in two off Eagle Harbour while attempting to put about; all but one of the life-boats were swept away before they could be launched; the captain permitted but nine persons, all passengers, to enter it, while himself, with eleven other passengers and all the crew, remained behind on the sinking vessel. "I will never leave this boat until the last soul is off," he said; "I am captain of her, and if she is a coffin for anybody she will be my coffin." It is pitiful to relate that but three out of the nine in the life-boat reached land alive. But the point to which we would call attention is that the captain carried an accident policy for £800 in the———, and it does not detract one iota from the value or courage of his sacrifice to say that without doubt his dying moments were sweetened by the thought that he was not leaving his family to be thrown penniless upon the world. It is a pleasure and an honour to be able to uphold the spirit and nerve the heart of such a man as Captain ———, and to protect his dear ones.

Wishes He Had.—Two men in ——— went out to ride a few days ago. When well under way, one of the reins got under the horse's tail. The animal became frisky, one of the men was thrown out, run over and badly bruised, and the other in attempting to release the rein was kicked in the forehead, cutting a deep gash. Both had been solicited to insure against accidents. One thought it was a "good thing" in general, but couldn't see how it was going to benefit him in particular. The other a short time ago signed an application for a £1,000 policy, but afterwards declined to take it. He now sees the moral and wishes he had insured.

Personals.

Mr. James R. Partridge (Ex-United States Minister), who committed suicide at Alicante, Spain, was insured in the *New York* Life for £3,000, and—under the provisions of that Company—the Policy is not invalidated by the manner of his death.

Mr. Charles Freeth.—We regret to announce the death, on the 2nd inst., after a very short illness, of Mr. Charles Freeth, who was connected with the *Sun* Fire Office since 1845.

Mr. G. H. McHenry has been appointed to the position of manager of the Royal Canadian of Montreal, to fill the vacancy caused by the death of Mr. Davison. Mr. McHenry was recently secretary to the Fire Insurance Association in Canada.

M. Flury.—A rumour that M. Flury, manager of La Metropole, had the intention of resigning is contradicted. M. Flury is at present in the United States looking after the Metropole's deposits on that side of the Atlantic.

Multum in Parvo.

☞ **BRITISH EMPIRE MUTUAL.**—At the annual meeting of the British Empire Mutual Life Assurance Company, held April 1st, the report, which was adopted, stated that the business for the past year amounted to £723,319, under 1,672 policies. Of these 271 for £176,555 were granted in exchange for the Lion Company's policies. The new annual premiums for the year were £26,313. After paying £22,800 as bonus, the sum of £53,682 had been added to the funds, which now amount to £956,623. It was also stated that the rate of mortality had again been below the estimate, and that the sum of £66,517 had been paid in claims.

☞ **NEW YORK.**—From the report of the New York Life Insurance Company for the year ending December 31, 1883, it appears that 15,561 new policies were issued, insuring £10,850,939; the accumulated fund on January 1, 1884, was £11,379,945; the income for the year was £2,717,599; and the surplus over all liabilities was £2,139,339.

☞ **LONDON AND LANCASHIRE.**—At the annual meeting of the London and Lancashire Life Assurance Company it was reported that the new assurances opened during the year amounted to £554,890, under 1,591 policies, giving a new premium income of £18,357. The net premium income for the year amounted to £102,853, and after payment of all outgoings, including cash bonuses to policy-holders, and dividends to shareholders at the rate of 15 per cent. on the original amount of capital paid up, the sum of £32,302 was added to the funds, which now stand at £332,628.

☞ **FIRE INSURANCE ASSOCIATION.** — At the annual meeting of the Fire Insurance Association it was reported that the net premiums, after deducting £54,350 for reinsurances, amounted to £244,129, and the losses, paid and outstanding, to £180,542. The balance carried forward to the credit of next year's account amounts to £20,373, and the total funds stand at £270,373.

BRITISH EMPIRE MUTUAL LIFE ASSURANCE COMPANY.

THE thirty-seventh annual general meeting of this company was held on Tuesday, the 1st inst., at the Cannon Street Hotel, E.C., under the presidency of Mr. John Runtz (chairman of the company).

The Secretary (Mr. Edwin Bowley) read the advertisement convening the meeting, as well as the directors' report as follows. The statement of accounts was taken as read.

The directors have much pleasure in presenting their report, which again records a satisfactory progress. In the financial year, 1883, 1,988 proposals were received, amounting to £850,600, resulting in 1,672 policies for £723,319; the new premiums payable thereon being £26,313 0s. 10d. Of these policies, 271 for £176,555 were granted in exchange for those issued by the Lion Life Assurance Company; 316 proposals for £127,331 were declined or not completed. In consideration of £2,453 17s. 6d. annuities have been granted for an annual payment of £341 7s. 3d. Four annuitants, in receipt of £131 16s., have died during the year. In the course of the same period 228 policy-holders have died, on whose lives 258 assurances had been effected; the claims thus arising, with bonuses, amounted to £66,517 10s. 5d., after paying cash bonuses to the extent of £21,254 17s. 6d., and reducing the premiums by £1,552 10s. The sum of £53,682 10s. 9d. has been added to the accumulated fund, which now amounts to £956,623 9s. 5d., held in securities of the highest class, and yielding interest exceeding £4 5s. per cent. The total income is £184,101 17s. 10d., the number of policies in force is 15,343, assuring £4,434,661; and the premiums payable thereon, £136,510 11s. 11d.

The new business introduced through the arrangement made with the Lion Life Company, and the mode in which this company has dealt with the Lion policy-holders, who have exchanged their policies, have proved to be satisfactory both in England and Canada. The claims still continue to fall below the estimated rate of mortality. As in former years, the securities have been carefully examined, and the accounts and balance-sheet for the year ending 31st December, 1883, have passed under the scrutiny of the auditors and been duly certified.

The directors record with much regret the decease of their highly esteemed colleague, Mr. Augustus Benham, who was the deputy-chairman of the company. Mr. Benham had been associated with the company for more than twenty-five years, and during that period had contributed most materially to its success. At an extraordinary meeting held on the 14th ult., Mr. William Henry Wills, M.P. for Coventry, was elected to the vacancy caused in the direction by the death of Mr. Benham.

The directors desire to call the attention of the members to the very considerable increase in the company's business, which has been made, moreover, without adding to the ratio of expenditure.

The directors congratulate the members on the very satisfactory addition of £53,682 10s. 9d. that has been made to the reserve fund, after payment during the year of £22,807 7s. 6d. to bonus policy-holders, and also that the accumulated fund is now close upon £1,000,000. They would point to this fact as a conclusive proof of the company's substantial position; and the satisfactory rate of progress that has been maintained over such a lengthened period justifies the anticipation of a thoroughly sound and prosperous future for the company.

The directors retiring by rotation are:—Messrs. Bompas, Freeman, Munro, and Runtz. The retiring auditor is Mr. Wm. Augustine Spain. All these gentlemen are eligible for re-election, and they offer themselves accordingly.

The Chairman desired, before proceeding to review the contents of the report, to express on behalf of the Board the deep sorrow and regret they felt at the loss they had sustained by the death of their colleague, Mr. Benham, referring in warm and eulogistic terms to the amiable, and at the same time thoroughly business-like qualities possessed by the late deputy-chairman. The vacancy so caused in the direction had been filled up, he was glad to say, by the election of Mr. William Henry Wills, M.P. for Coventry, at a special meeting held on the 14th of last month. Three candidates had offered themselves; but the other two gentlemen, believing Mr. Wills to be capable of rendering greater service than themselves, had most gracefully retired in his favour. (Hear, hear.) The report now before the meeting, the Chairman proceeded to say, was the thirty-seventh annual report of the Company. As the meeting had already heard, the office had received during the year just closed 1,988 proposals of assurance for £850,650, resulting in the issue of 1,672 policies, assuring the sum of £723,319. The new premiums paying thereon amounted to

£26,313 0s. 10d. That sum represented a great advance on previous years. (Hear, hear.) Taking the last five years, it would be found that in 1879 the new assurances amounted to £276,266, in 1880 to £320,042, in 1881 to £420,168, in 1882 to £404,515, and in 1883 to £723,319, being an increase over last year's new business of £318,734. Now, it was necessary to explain the special circumstances which had led, in great measure, to that large increase. During the past year the Board had taken over the policy-holders of the Lion Company—a new life assurance office which had commenced business in 1880, and had carried it on until 1883. At that date, however, the Company had deemed it advisable to give up life business and to carry on only their fire branch, which they were now doing. He particularly wished the meeting to understand that, in taking over the Lion, they were not taking over an old company with old lives, because the average age of the policies was only fifteen months, while the average age of the policy-holders was only 37 years. In all other respects, too, the transfer differed in character to that generally obtained in such cases, where the proprietors alone effected the change without any consideration for the policy-holders. In this case, however, all the policy-holders had been personally asked whether they were willing to exchange a Lion policy for a British Empire policy; so that, really, it had been a voluntary transfer on the part of the assured themselves. Moreover, this company had taken over from the Lion such proportion of the premiums already paid by the policy-holders as had been considered right and just by the actuary. Therefore it was necessary to remember that of the 1,672 new policies issued by the office, 271 had been transferred from the Lion, representing assurances to the amount of £176,555. Deducting that amount from the total of £723,319 a balance was left of £546,764 as the actual new business of the year, and which in making a comparison was to be contrasted with the £404,585 of the year before The new premiums of the year amounted to £26,313, while the total income of the company from premiums, less re-insurances, was £134,872, being an increase over last year of £15,769. The total income of the company from all sources amounted to £184,101 17s. 10d. The claims paid during the year, with bonus additions, had been £66,517 10s. 5d., arising from 228 deaths, and in respect of 258 policies. The deaths last year had numbered 195. Thus, this year there had been 33 more deaths than in 1882. On the other hand, in 1881, there had been 230 deaths, or two more than during the past year. The deaths expected by the H.M. tables—which were the tables used by the office—should have been 271; so that the deaths this past year, although 33 more than the year before, were really 43 below the number provided for by the tables' of mortality. Reviewing the experience of the company from the commencement to the end of 1882, it would be found that their average death rate was about 16 per cent. below the numbers provided for in the mortality tables, while this year it had been as much as 19 per cent. below the actuarial expectation. (Hear, hear.) The company had now on risk 13,815 lives, assured by 15,343 policies, while the total sum assured amounted to £4,434,661. In regard to the accumulated fund it would afford the policy-holders satisfaction to note that after payment of all claims, and returning to the assured the sum of £22,807, partly in cash bonus and partly in bonus reduction of premiums, the Board had been able to add to the fund the handsome sum of £53,682. The invested funds of the Company had realised during the past year over £4 5s. per cent.; but, as it would be readily understood there must always be a considerable amount in the shape of "interest accrued but not paid," "cash on current account," "agency balances," and "outstanding premiums," which it was not possible to place in an interest-earning position. Setting aside this unremunerative portion of the funds it would be found that their actual investments earned as much as £4 7s. 6d. per cent. In conclusion the Chairman observed that it afforded the Directors extreme pleasure to come before the policy-holders and present them with so favourable a report. He then formally moved the adoption of the report and accounts.

Mr. W. H. Wills, M.P., seconded the resolution, and said that the circumstance reminded him of the occasion when, fifteen years ago, he had last risen to perform that duty. At that meeting, the chairman of the day had congratulated the members on the satisfactory character of the report then submitted, although, at that time, the total income of the Company had not exceeded £90,000, whereas it now amounted to over £184,000. Thus, in little more than fourteen years, the business of the office had doubled itself. No doubt a great part of this satisfactory rate of progress was due to the wider recognition among the public at large, of not only the advantage, but also the desirability of life assurance. Moreover, the Company's marked success was attributable to the great and increasing favour with which the principle of mutual assurance was regarded. Doubtless, a mutual office in the early days of its establishment, suffered in a measure from want of backbone inasmuch as it lacked the support given to a proprietary company by the proprietor's capital. For this reason, many people preferred an old proprietary office to a young and comparatively inexperienced mutual office; but this company at least could claim to have long since emerged from that stage, and possessing, as it now did an ample reserve fund, it could offer an amount of security not to be rivalled by the oldest proprietary office in the kingdom. (Hear, hear.) As up to the present he had had no part in the management of the Company, he could freely express his views concerning its character. The insight he had obtained into the Company's affairs had convinced and satisfied him on at least two points, namely, that the business of the office was administered in a business-like manner by business men, and next, that the policy-holders were invariably treated with consideration and liberality. (Hear, hear.)

Mr. Lindsay, echoing, he believed, the opinion of all present, desired to express his entire satisfaction with the Directors' report, and with the explanatory comments of the Chairman. (Hear, hear.)

The resolution was then put and passed unanimously.

Dr. J. H. Trouncer (Deputy-chairman) next moved the re-election of the retiring Directors, viz.:—Messrs. Bompas, Freeman, Munro, and Runtz, each resolution being proposed separately, and duly carried.

The Chairman returned the thanks of his colleagues and himself and stated that the greatest possible care was exercised by the board in the disposition of the Companys' funds, and in the selection of lives proposed for assurance. (Hear, hear.) He trusted that they might yet enjoy many more years in the Company's service. (Hear, hear.)

A resolution was next moved, seconded, and agreed to, re-appointing Mr. W. A. Spain as auditor.

This gentleman, in acknowledging the compliment, assured the members as to the particular care with which he and his colleague audited the Company's accounts, and duly examined every quarter all the deeds and documents relating to the Company's investments. (Hear, hear.)

A vote of thanks to the Chairman brought the meeting to an end.

REVENUE ACCOUNT FOR YEAR ENDING 31st DECEMBER, 1883.

REVENUE.

To amount of funds at the beginning of the year		£902,940	18 8
„ Life premiums.. .. £136,510 11 11			
Less re-assurances .. 1,637 18 11			
		134,872	13 0
„ Consideration for annuities granted ..		2,453	17 0
„ Interest and dividends .. £40,139 10 5			
Less Income tax .. 789 6 0			
		39,350	4 5
„ Fines and fees		150	4 2
„ Profit on sale of stock		4,847	13 10
		£1,084,615	11 7

EXPENDITURE.

By claims		£66,517	10 5
„ Endowments		2,992	8 4
„ Annuities		2,093	2 5
„ Surrenders		6,233	7 0
„ Cash bonus		21,254	17 6
„ Bonus reduction of premiums ..		1,552	10 0
„ Commission		8,566	19 5
„ Expenses of management		18,781	7 1
„ Amount of funds at the end of the year (as per Second Schedule) ..		956,623	9 5
		£1,084,615	11 7

BALANCE SHEET, 31ST DECEMBER, 1883.

LIABILITIES.

	£	s.	d.
To claims admitted but not paid	18,404	6	6
., Tradesmen's accounts	2,484	18	2
,, Loan fees account	1,116	9	8
,, Assurance fund	956,623	9	5
	£978,629	3	9

ASSETS.

	£	s.	d.
By mortgages on property within the United Kingdom	352,221	7	3
Freehold land and ground rents	135,873	13	8
Loans on the Company's policies	72,562	2	5
Loans on personal security	12,738	10	5
Investments :—			
£10,729 Consols	10,220	3	3
22,000 Queensland Bonds	22,000	0	0
17,800 Tasmanian Bonds ..	17,491	0	0
23,500 South Australian Bonds ..	23,731	5	0
13,500 Canadian Bonds	13,310	12	6
11,500 Victoria Bonds	12,100	0	0
14,800 New South Wales Bonds ..	14,740	12	6
63,400 Cape of Good Hope Bonds ..	62,757	0	0
9,500 New Brunswick Bonds ..	9,481	0	0
12,000 Montreal Bonds	11,155	0	0
1,000 British Columbia Bonds ..	1,000	0	0
12,000 Toronto Bonds	12,907	0	0
12,000 Winnipeg Bonds	13,298	15	0
5,000 Ottawa Bonds	5,843	15	0
7,500 Swedish Bonds	7,629	7	6
13,700 Great Eastern Railway ..	9,975	7	6
9,184 North-Eastern Railway ..	15,615	6	9
3,000 North-Western Railway	5,148	1	0
3,570 Great Western Railway	4,999	18	6
7,500 Furness Railway	9,650	6	3
10,580 Bombay and Baroda Railway ..	11,047	12	3
5,000 Northern of Canada Railway ..	5,113	15	0
12,000 Globe Telegraph Pref. Shares ..	14,964	17	6
Interest accrued but unpaid	5,756	16	2
Cash on deposit	3,000	0	0
Cash on current account and in hand ..	6,897	18	5
Agency balances	12,519	0	8
Outstanding premiums (payable in January)	26,611	9	3
	£978,629	3	9

WESTERN COUNTIES AND LONDON MUTUAL LIFE ASSURANCE COMPANY.

THE annual meeting of the Western Counties and London Mutual Life Assurance Company was held on March 31st, at the chief offices of the Company, 20, Princess-square, Plymouth. The Chairman (Mr. C. F. Tubbs) occupied the chair, and there were also present Messrs. F. A Morrish, J. May, and John Shelly, Mr. W. J. White, secretary, and a number of shareholders.

The Secretary read the Annual Report of the Directors and the Accounts, and also the Certificate of the Auditor, Mr. Samuel Knight, of London, who certified that the books and accounts of the Company had been carefully and accurately kept. The Report was as follows :—

The Directors have the pleasure of presenting the following Report for the year ending January 31st, 1884. During the year 127 proposals have been received for the sum of £61,375 ; of these 283 policies have been granted assuring £41,300, and producing a new annual premium income of £1,276 9s. The claims and matured endowments paid and admitted amounted to £6,823 17s. 10d., which was assured under 48 policies, the mortality being below the average of the last five years. As the result of conducting the business through the head office in Plymouth only, which you may remember the Directors last year announced their intention of doing, a large reduction in expenditure has been effected. The Directors intend to persevere in this policy, and anticipate their being able to effect a much larger reduction during the coming year. Although the amount of business done has been smaller, the Directors are glad to announce an increase of the accumulated funds of £4,040, a sum above the average of the past ten years. The Directors regret having to record the death during the past year of one of their number, Mr. Thomas H. Griffith, and also

of Mr. Samuel Jackson, their auditor in Plymouth, both of whom had been associated with the Company for a number of years. The Directors intend to propose, at an extraordinary meeting to be held immediately after this meeting, that vacancies occurring in the directorate may remain unfilled, provided that the number be not reduced below three. The retiring Directors, Mr. C. F. Tubbs and Mr. Alderman Shelly, and the Auditor, M. S. Knight, are eligible, and offer themselves for re-election. It will also be necessary to elect an auditor to fill the vacancy caused by Mr. Samuel Jackson's death. The Directors cordially invite the co-operation of the policy-holders in promoting and extending the business of this Company.

The Chairman proposed the adoption of the report and the accounts, and said it gave him pleasure to do so, since the result of the year's working seemed to justify the decided step taken last year in removing the whole of the business to the Plymouth office. The Directors had exercised the greatest care in the selection of lives, so as to secure good business only, and the claims were lower than they might have expected, seeing that the Company was another year older. The claims had been less and the mortality below the average of the past five years. That was a gratifying feature in the business this year, and although the amount of new business was smaller, the expenses of management had been so reduced that £4,000 had been added to their accumulated capital. (Hear, hear.) They missed the faces of two gentlemen who had always been present at their annual meetings—Mr. T. H. Griffith, of London, who for many years was associated with them in the directorate ; and their well-known and highly-esteemed late townsman, Mr. Samuel Jackson, who had belonged to the Company from the commencement. Under ordinary circumstances a director would be elected to fill the vacancy caused by the death of Mr. Griffith but as their policy was to curtail expenses wherever practicable, it was intended to propose at a meeting to be held directly after that one, that vacancies in the directorate should be allowed to remain unfilled provided the number be not reduced below three. He had little more to lay before them with regard to the accounts, but the directors asked for their continued confidence, their loyal support, and their earnest co-operation. Theirs was a mutual society, and all participated in whatever success was achieved, and their success must be measured mainly by the interest taken in the Company by existing policy-holders. The Directors had effected a great improvement in the liabilities of the Company. They stood upon a sure basis and were not afraid to come before the public and say they would like that basis to be built upon, and those who formed that basis had it in their power to do much towards raising the superstructure. He hoped that meeting would send a beating pulse of energy through their whole society. (Hear, hear.)

Mr. J. May, J.P., of Devonport, in seconding the adoption of the report and accounts, said the directors had come to the determination to keep down the expenses in every possible way, and especially in the large outlay they used to incur for getting new business. This matter had, however, given them considerable anxiety, and in addition to the experience they were able to bring to the consideration of the matter, their conclusions had been confirmed by independent opinions of the best authority. (Hear, hear.) The large addition to their accumulated profits during the past year was very encouraging, and by cutting down expenses and by the amount of new business that would come in the course of the year the directors hoped to show a still larger amount of accumulated funds at the next meeting. The wisdom of doing away with the London office had been fully proved, and he looked forward with great hope to the future, because although their business might not be so large in amount they were confident it would be a safe business, and one upon which the policy-holders could rely as affording them ample security for their stake in the society. (Hear, hear.)

The report and accounts were then adopted unanimously.

Mr. F. A. Morrish, J.P., proposed the re-election of Mr. C. F. Tubbs (the chairman) and Mr. John Shelly as directors. Mr. Morrish thought the indebtedness of the Company to these two gentlemen, especially during the last two or three years, should be publicly recognised. They had the utmost confidence in Mr. Tubbs and Mr. Shelly, and knew they would not put their hands to anything that would not tend towards prosperity and success. (Hear, hear.)

Mr. R. N. Worth seconded the proposition, and endorsed, as a policy-holder, what Mr. Morrish had said as a director; and Mr. Tubbs and Mr. Shelly were then unanimously re-elected.

The Chairman, in acknowledging his re-election, said he had that day more confidence than ever in the business of the Company, and could say with even more pleasure that that business was worthy of the attention and support of the public. (Hear, hear.) They had freed the business from all detrimental encumbrance; and it now rested with the policy-holders to make it a large Company if they liked, and they would themselves reap the benefit of increased prosperity. The Chairman then alluded to the absence of the deputy-chairman, Mr. J. Plimsaul, who had been unwell, but who, he was glad to say, there was a prospect would soon be amongst them again.

Mr. Shelly also returned thanks for re-election.

The Chairman next proposed the re-election of the auditor, Mr. Samuel Knight, of London, who, he said, gave them very valuable assistance concerning matters in London. —This proposition having been seconded by Mr. W. A. Clark, and unanimously agreed to, the Chairman proceeded to move the election of Mr. John Smith as second auditor in the place of the late Mr. Samuel Jackson. The Chairman remarked that Mr. Smith was a man of business of a strict and diligent character, and a policy-holder of many years standing.

Mr. Shelly seconded the election of Mr. Smith, believing that his appointment would be received with great satisfaction, and have the entire confidence of the policy-holders.

Mr. Smith, having been unanimously elected, said he had not sought the post, but having been elected he would accept the office, and endeavour to discharge it to the best of his ability. He proceeded to offer some remarks upon the recent changes in the management of the Company's business, which changes he highly commended. He also expressed his great confidence in the Directors of the Company, who, he remarked, were all well known as men of honour and business character. (Hear, hear.) All the policy-holders could assure their friends they were absolutely safe in taking out policies in that Company. (Applause.)

The Chairman next proposed a vote of thanks to the medical officers, Dr. Prance and Mr. J. May, jun., both of whom he highly eulogised.

Mr. Morrish seconded the proposition, and when it had been passed Dr. Prance acknowledged the compliment. He expressed satisfaction at the fact that the claims upon the Company last year were smaller than usual, and said the medical officers fully appreciated the fact that the carrying on of an insurance business in a remunerative way must depend upon the character of the lives insured. There were some companies whose great idea was to get a big business, but their policy was not so much to get a big business as a safe business. (Hear, hear.)

A vote of thanks to the officers of the Company was also proposed by the Chairman. Mr. White, the secretary, he said, had filled that position with very great credit to himself and very much satisfaction to the Directors, and the staff under him were very faithful and diligent, and fully to be relied upon.

Mr. May, in seconding the vote of thanks, said that since Mr. White had filled the office of secretary he had fully justified the opinion the Directors had formed of him before as a man of diligent habits and high moral qualities.

The Secretary, in acknowledging the compliment on behalf of himself and the staff, said his duties were rendered all the more pleasant by the cheerful and judicious counsel of the Chairman. The policy-holders might not know the amount of time the Chairman gave to the duties. Every day he was at the office, and was familiar with every detail of the work; and the other Directors were also ever ready to serve the policy-holders. He (Mr. White) was ably seconded by every officer of the Company and by the agents, who, he believed, would recognise in that meeting a reason for further exerting themselves to extend the business of the Company.

The meeting was then made special, and it was resolved, on the motion of the Chairman, seconded by Mr. Shelly, to alter the rule so that vacancies in the directorate may remain unfilled so long as the number of Directors is not reduced below three.

A vote of thanks to the chairman brought the meeting to a close.

NATIONAL LIFE ASSURANCE SOCIETY.

DIRECTORS' REPORT.

THE Directors have pleasure in presenting to the Fifty-fourth Annual General Court of the National Life Assurance Society, the usual yearly Statements made up to 31st December, 1883, in accordance with the provisions of the "Assurance Companies Act, 1870."

It will be seen from the Revenue Account that the claims have been heavy: the Policies on which they have arisen, were, however, for the most part, of old standing; and it is only in Class A that the actual claims have exceeded the expectation. In Classes B and C they have been considerably within the expected amount.

The claims in Class A were, indeed, £35,000 more in 1883 than in 1882; but the total payments under this head for the three years which have elapsed since the last division of profit have nevertheless been only £600 in excess of the expectation; the mortality in the two previous years having been very favourable.

The new Assurances effected in 1883 were somewhat less than those in the previous year; and this fact, taken in conjunction with an unusually large number of lapsed Policies, has reduced the Premium Income for 1883 by £1,600, as compared with that of the previous year. Taking into account the allowance of £22,082 applied during the past year in reduction of Premiums, the Assurance Fund is thus less, by £15,633, than the amount at which it stood on 31st December, 1882. That Fund, however, still stands higher by £31,054 than at the end of 1881, while the liability has materially decreased on account of a large number of Policies having lapsed.

The Funds of the Society, as invested on 31st December, 1883, were yielding Interest at the average rate of £4 14s. 9d. per cent. per annum.

The Directors have reason to believe that the recent alterations in the Rules and practice of the Society have been very cordially approved, especially that by which, while the fullest security was provided, the unlimited liability of individual Members was abolished; and that by which claims are now payable in 30 days, instead of three months, after admission of the proof of death.

In the new Prospectus, the members will doubtless have observed statements with reference to the moderate fixed rates of Premium for Military and Naval Officers, covering every risk incidental to the exercise of their profession, in Peace or War, in any part of the World: as well as to the arrangements for Trust Policies under the Married Women's Property Act, 1882: and to the option of taking Annuities instead of the sums assured, given under Table III. The Directors desire to recommend these schemes to the careful consideration of the Members and the Public, believing that they offer great advantages to Assurers.

The Directors retiring from office on the present occasion are George Burnand, Esq., The Hon. Gerald C. Talbot, and Sir Henry W. Tyler: and the retiring Auditor is Lewis C. Berger, Esq. These gentlemen offer themselves for re-election.

It is with great regret that the Directors have announced the resignation by Mr. Lock of the seat at the Board which he has held during the last thirteen years; the state of his health precluding the hope of his again taking an active part in their deliberations.

The vacancy so caused will be filled up at the Annual General Court, to be held on the 2nd of April.

Under the new rule the next valuation for the division of profit will be made either at the end of 1884 or 1885, at the discretion of the Court of Directors. In either case, the profit will be applied in and after the year 1886.

The Directors look forward with confidence to a result from that valuation which will be thoroughly satisfactory to the Members of the Society in every Class; and they trust that their own constant efforts to promote the well-being of the Society, and to extend its sphere of usefulness, will be heartily supported by all who are interested in its proceedings.

By order of the Court of Directors,
HENRY JOHN PUCKLE,
Secretary.

12th March, 1884.

THE ACTUARY, No. 34.

Mr. Edwin James Farren.

One of the most able writers on Life Contingencies which this or any other country has produced.

He was trained in the *Asylum* Life, under his father; and on the retirement of the latter, he was appointed Actuary; but the Company was then verging upon the fate which so speedily befell it.

In 1855 he was appointed Actuary and Secretary of the *Gresham*, and remained in that position until September, 1864.

In 1844, he published "Historical Essay on the Rise and Early Progress of the Doctrine of Life Contingencies in England, leading to the establishment of the first Life Assurance Society, in which ages were distinguished." A pamphlet full of interest and instruction, from which we frequently quote in these pages.

In 1850, he published "Life Contingency Table." Part I. "The Chances of Premature Death, and the Value of Selection amongst Assured Lives;" a quarto pamphlet of considerable rarity.

In addition to the preceding, the following papers will be found in the *Assurance Magazine.*

1851.—"On Indirect Methods of acquiring Knowledge; the Method of History; the first Table of Mortality."

,, "Letters on Life Contingency Problems."

1853.—"On the Reliability of Data, when tested by the conclusions to which they lead."

,, Letter—"On the Period intervening between the Date of Death and Payment of Sum Assured."

,, "On the Form of the Number whose Logarithm is equal to itself."

,, Letter — "Proper Expression for the Amount of £1, with a Fractional Part of a Year's Interest."

,, Letter — "The Chances of Premature Death among Select Lives."

,, Letter—"On the Inadequacy of Existing Data for Determining the Rate of Mortality among Select Lives.

1855.—"On the Improvement of Life Contingency Calculations."

,, Letter—"On the Application of the Differential and Integral Calculus to 'Interest' Questions."

,, "On the Valuation of Government Securities."

1858.—"On the Improvement of Life Contingency Calculations." Part II. "The System of Dependent Risks."

1859.—Letter—"Professor Silvester's Lectures.

Every line written by Mr. Farren is worthy of the attentive study of students.

He gave evidence before the Select Parliamentary Committee on Assurance Association, 1853.

In the autumn of 1864, the death of Mr. Farren, suddenly, was reported; this was founded on a misapprehension.—*Insurance Cyclopædia.*

◆

Fate in League with the Accident Company.—From the legion of recent elevator accidents we select one which bears with singular directness on the remark we have so often made, that the possession of an accident policy seems actually to lessen the danger of its holder. Several gentlemen were ascending in the hydraulic elevator of the ——— Hotel, at ———, ———, Nov. 11, when the running gear proved to be out of order so that its ascent could not be stopped. All jumped off in safety except Mr. T. E. R———, a well-known and highly popular commercial traveller for a ——— house, who was caught by the left arm and leg, and before he could be extricated his skull was literally crushed to fragments and his neck broken. He leaves a wife and two children, and till the 1st of March last had held a policy in the ———, but had let it lapse, promising to renew it last autumn. Among the other passengers were two gentlemen—Mr. D. S. M———, a prominent commercial traveller, and Mr. J. C. B———, of ———, each carrying £1,000 insurance with the ——— Company, and who were entirely unhurt.

◆

A Spirit of Airs and Waters.

From the reek of the pond, a lily
   Has risen in raiment white—
A spirit of airs and waters—
   A form of incarnate light;
      Yet, except for the rooted stem
      That steadies her diadem,
Except for the earth she is nourished by,
Could the soul of the lily have climbed to the sky?

TERMS OF SUBSCRIPTION.
ANNUAL Subscription (including postage), Paid in advance, 9s.

NOTICE TO CORRESPONDENTS.
All Communications intended for insertion to be addressed to the Editor, " The INSURANCE SPECTATOR OF LONDON," 5, Ludgate Circus Buildings, E.C.

CONTENTS:

THE

Insurance Spectator of London.
APRIL 15, 1884.

We have pleasure in calling attention to the advertisement in this issue of the *Union* Plate Glass Insurance Company. Though founded so recently as May, 1882, the Company has already established three hundred agencies throughout the country, many of whom have laid the foundation of a good business. The *Union* has a branch office in Hamburg, under Government sanction, and the results up to the end of last year were satisfactory to the Board. There is a strong upward tendency in the income of the Company, and a downward tendency in the expenditure. In the appointment of Mr. Alfred John Proud to the position of Manager, the Directors have secured the services of a gentleman of experience and energy, and the Company is already feeling the advantage of Mr. Proud's administrative abilities. We have no hesitation in endorsing the *Union*, sound, progressive, and reliable.

———————

THE report of the Annual Meeting of the *Western Counties and London* Mutual Life Assurance Company on page 121 is full of interest, and indicates a marked step in real progress. When a large reduction in expenditure is accompanied by an abnormal addition to the reserves, it is evident that the management is alive to the requirements of modern Life Insurance, and equal also to the demands. Founded nearly a quarter of a century since, the *Western Counties and London* has always possessed a character for readiness and despatch in the settlement of claims as they arose. In its constitution, *mutual*, no portion of the profits realized is diverted from the policy-holders, while the security is absolutely beyond challenge. An all-round effort this year will do very much to make the *Western Counties and London* as largely patronized as its strong financial position and liberal programme justify and support.

———————

THE New Insurances of the *British Empire* Mutual Life Assurance Company for 1883 are practically Three Quarters of a Million Sterling. Such a result means immense activity alike at the Head Office and the Branches. Mr. Bowley is evidently well supported by his Agencies. The truth is, the Company is a good one to work for, and has, moreover, come to the front of late years in a very remarkable manner. The following clause in the (37th Annual) Report so succinctly sets forth the *cause* of the Company's popularity and success, that we make no apology for reproducing it. "The Directors congratulate the Members on the very satisfactory addition of £53,682 10s. 9d. that has been made to the Reserve Fund, after payment during the year of £22,807 7s. 6d. to Bonus Policy-holders, and also that the Accumulated Fund is now close upon £1,000,000. They would point to this fact as a conclusive proof of the Company's substantial position; and the satisfactory rate of progress that has been maintained over such a lengthened period justifies the anticipation of a thoroughly sound and prosperous future for the Company."

AT the Annual General Court of the National Life Assurance Society, on the 2nd inst., the Directors' Report, which appears on page 122, was submitted and adopted. The Society was founded more than half a century since, and unites the advantages of age, with the modern developments which are safe as well as attractive. A very valuable feature is the payment of claims in thirty days (instead of three months) after proof of death has been supplied. The concluding sentences of the Report have interest for, and should at once influence, intending insurers, and also those who have wisely selected the *National* for the protection of their homes. It runs thus:—"Under the new rule the next valuation for the division of profit will be made either at the end of 1884 or 1885, at the discretion of the Court of Directors. In either case, the profit will be applied in and after the year 1886." "The Directors look forward with confidence to a result from that valuation which will be thoroughly satisfactory to the Members of the Society in every class; and they trust that their own constant efforts to promote the well-being of the Society, and to extend its sphere of usefulness, will be heartily supported by all who are interested in its proceedings." We have only to add that the assets of the Society exceed eight hundred and forty thousand pounds, and that, in point of strength and freedom from vexatious restrictions the *National* has no superior and few equals.

———————

"A FAIR field and no favour," is a sentiment which might well be observed in reference to the two American Life Offices represented in this Country. The tone adopted by the Trans-Atlantic Press concerning English Offices represented on the other side, has always been one of the greatest friendliness. The following *excerpt* from our namesake of New York, is a fair specimen of the tone in which English Offices are referred to by our American Cousins.—"It looks now as if the English companies which are erecting their own buildings in this country had come to stay. The Liverpool and London and Globe, Royal, Commercial Union, Imperial and Queen each own a handsome building of their own in this city, and the Imperial is about to erect another in Chicago. The Commercial Union has its own building in Philadelphia, and we shall doubtless hear of others by other companies ere long. This is an evidence of faith in American business not to be slighted." We are led to these remarks in connection with the figures of the *New York* Life for 1883. We are accustomed to big figures in connection with leading American Companies, but the announcement that the Insurances of the *New York* Life for last year nearly reached Eleven Millions sterling, fairly takes one's breath away. The Income of the Company is now close upon Two and three-quarter Millions sterling, and the surplus over all liabilities considerably in excess of Two Millions sterling. The Company is in every way one of the soundest and most prosperous Life Offices in existence.

THREE CURIOSITIES.

(ADVERTISED GRATIS.)

THE JOHN BULL INSURANCE COMPANY (LIMITED). —For fire and marine insurance. Incorporated under the Companies Act, 1862 and 1867. Capital, £100,000. Chief offices: 6, Grocers' Hall Court, Poultry, London, E.C. Agencies in the principal towns in England. Directors: Samuel Crosse, Esq.; Benjamin Gregory, Esq.; Frederick R. Harold, Esq.; Samuel Wells, Esq. Bankers: Messrs. G. Barker and Co., 39 and 40, Mark Lane, E.C. Solicitors: Messrs. Godfrey and Robertson, 53 and 54, Chancery Lane, W.C. Manager (*pro tem.*): F. R. Harold.

THE CITY AND PROVINCIAL INSURANCE COMPANY (LIMITED).—Incorporated under the Joint Stock Companies Acts, 1862 to 1880. Registered capital, £25,000. Fire insurance department. Directors: Thomas Oldham, Esq.; Cornelius Nicolls, Esq.; Henry Peplow, Esq.; D. Finlay, Esq. Solicitor: J. H. Boardman, Esq. Manager and secretary: F. W. Dawson. Head office: 9, Corporation-Street, Manchester.

THE OAK INSURANCE COMPANY (LIMITED).— Incorporated under the Joint Stock Companies Acts, 1862 to 1882. Non Tariff. Directors: R. W. Hopkins, Esq., Longsight; J. T. Lockey, Esq., Cable Street, Rochdale Road; W. Stanley, Esq. (Stanley and Wainwright), Swan Street; W. Mercer, Esq., Princess Street; all of Manchester. Manager and Secretary: S. E. Gibbons. Head office: 75, Bridge Street, Manchester.

The Campaign of 1884 has thus far been a sanguinary one, but the victims have in every case been promptly cared for, and the survivors of the dead bless their memory the more fevently for the prudent foresight which made provision for their need. The whole accident claims paid would make more than 1,000 pages, and fill twenty-five issues of the INSURANCE SPECTATOR.

INSURANCE AND ASSURANCE.

SOLOMON KEENBRIAR and his nephew, Ralph, dropped down upon the people of Scufflescruff as if from the clouds, and immediately took the rank due to their seemingly celestial origin.

Spinsters who acknowledged thirty or upwards set their caps for the uncle, whilst those who acknowledged nothing, chronologically speaking, turned their attention to the nephew.

The Keenbriars took a house, which they kept in approved bachelor style. Scufflescruff was a cheap place to live in, but the uncle and nephew must have had money, even there, to hold up their heads as they did.

I was a young lawyer, sitting in my office, when one day the elder and younger Keenbriar entered.

"Mr. McJorkle," said Keenbriar, senior, "we have called to consult you on an important legal question."

"Ah?" I answered.

"I wish to insure my nephew's life. Can I do so?" he asked.

"Have you an insurable interest?" I inquired. The pair exchanged glances.

"What do, you mean?" returned the uncle.

"Does your nephew owe you anything?" I replied.

There was another change of glances.

"He does," said Mr. Keenbriar, beaming kindly at his nephew, who cast down his eyes and blushed.

"Of course I intend to leave him everything, but should I chance to outlive him, which is not very likely, I might as well have what is due to me out of some good company."

"There is no doubt of your right to insure under the circumstances," I answered. "How much does you nephew owe you?"

"£2,000," said the old gentleman; and the nephew nodded.

I advised that the insurance be effected in the Wigglesworth Company, which was the best I knew, and it was done accordingly.

Ralph Keenbriar was then thirty years old, and, at that age, according to the tables, a man has precisely eleven years and six hundred and eighty-two thousandths of a year to live—not that any man ever did live exactly that length of time after reaching thirty; but that is the fine point down to which the insurance companies have figured it, and if one dies before or after his time comes, it isn't their fault.

Now, it wasn't three months after young Keenbriar's life was insured, till he went out trouting one day on a neighbouring lake. He didn't return, but the boat was found upset, and his hat floating on the water.

For days and days they dragged the lake. At last the body was found. The features were past recognition, but the garments were those Ralph was known to have worn, and papers in the pockets of the corpse left no doubt of its identity.

I don't think I ever had so sorrowful a client as Mr. Keenbriar was the day he placed in my hands, for collection, the policy on his nephew's life.

"Mr.—Mr. McJorkle," he sobbed, " pl — please see to this. Poor Ralph!" he faltered, turning away his head. "I cannot bear to think of it."

I came as near weeping as a lawyer can—when not before a jury—over a pure matter of business.

I took the paper, put in the preliminary proofs and notice, but the company, as usual, was obdurately sceptical, and declined to pay.

I sued. They defended; and, on the trial, attempted to prove that the body found was a trifle shorter than the recorded measurement of Dick Cabbage, the tailor, who had made poor Ralph's last suit. But the other evidence was so strong that the jury after making due allowance for shrinkage, deemed the variance immaterial, and gave a verdict for the plaintiff.

Without interrupting the current of my story, I could not well bring in till now the fact that Mr. Keenbriar, a few days after the issuing of the policy, got me to draft his will, leaving all of which he might die possessed to his "beloved nephew Ralph."

Ralph, you see by consulting the tables, being only thirty, while his uncle was sixty, had just three years and eight hundred and sixty-two thousandths longer to live than the latter—a very good reason for making a will in favour of the nephew. I took it as a great compliment that Mr. Keenbriar named me his sole executor.

Solomon Keenbriar's health broke down after his nephew's death, and within a year he, too, was gathered to his fathers in spite of the figures in the table. I was surprised to find his will unaltered, seeing that the sole legatee had died before the testator; but a glance at the condition of the estate put an end to my astonishment. Mr. Keenbriar's assets turned out to be so nearly nothing, that it was plain he had not thought it worth the trouble to make another will.

Through an advertisement in a foreign paper, I was put upon the track of a large estate left by a millionaire, who had died shortly before Solomon Keenbriar, and of whom the latter, though but a distant relative, proved to be the next-of-kin. This fortune, of course, came into my hands, as executor, and would have now belonged to the drowned nephew had he still survived. As it was, I could only publish notice that the heirs-at-law of Solomon Keenbriar, by calling at my address, "would hear of something to their advantage."

I was detained at my office till a late hour one night. I had sent away the boy, and was seated alone at my desk, when a stranger entered and stood unexpectedly before me.

I had never believed much in ghosts, but when I found myself face to face with the dead and gone Ralph Keenbriar, whose death had been irrevocably established by the verdict of a jury, I started in amazement.

"Good evening, Mr. McJorkle," said the apparition, not in the least disconcerted.

"Good evening," I managed to answer, faintly.

"I see by the papers that my uncle is dead."

"And so I supposed you were," I replied.

"Not quite," cheerily returned the visitor.

"But I proved it to the jury," said I.

"More fools they."

"And the body found?"

"It was bought from a resurrectionist, dressed in my clothes, and sunk in the lake by filling the pockets with sand."

"So the whole thing was an infamous fraud!" I exclaimed, in profound disgust.

The answer was a shrug and a chuckle.

"I need scarcely inquire the object of your visit," I added.

"Of course not—it is to demand the money in your hands."

For a moment I hesitated. Should I call a policeman and hand the scoundrel over to justice, or stand loyally by the obligation between a lawyer and his client? The doubt lasted but an instant.

"You shall have the money," I answered, "but it must be on one condition."

"And that is——"

"That you leave sufficient in my hands to reimburse the insurance company for the sum of which it was defrauded."

After a little demurring, the proposition was accepted.

I never saw Ralph Keenbriar again, and the next day the Wrigglesworth Insurance Company mysteriously received two thousand pounds, with arrears of interest, deducting the premium paid, to be credited as "conscience money."

LAW INTELLIGENCE.

CHANCERY DIVISION.
(*Before* MR. JUSTICE CHITTY.)

IN RE NORTHERN COUNTIES OF ENGLAND FIRE INSURANCE COMPANY (LIMITED).

This was a summons taken out by the liquidator of the company, with the object of obtaining a declaration that Mr. Halliwell and other directors of the company were liable to repay money said to have been improperly paid out of capital. It appeared that between 1877 and 1880 balance-sheets were published which declared the company to be in a prosperous state, but subsequently the concern went into liquidation, and, the balance-sheets being found to be fraudulent, Mr. Halliwell and some of the other directors were prosecuted, and convicted. The liquidator, having settled with some of the directors, who were anxious to pay as far as they were able, sought also to make the other directors refund what had been improperly paid.

Mr. Romer, Q.C., and Mr. Oswald appeared for the liquidator, and Mr. Bramwell Davis for Mr. Halliwell.

His lordship said it had been proved up to the hilt that the balance-sheets were false, and there was a joint and several liability for the sums paid. He therefore made the declaration asked for, and ordered an inquiry as to the loss sustained by the company.

Life Insurance once entered upon, it should be regarded as a religious duty to continue to meet the annual charge with promptness and alacrity, as a new contribution to a fund gradually but surely destined to make happy and comfortable the objects of his love and care when he is lost to their presence and aid.

PLATE GLASS INSURANCE COMPANIES.

YORKSHIRE PROVIDENT LIFE ASSURANCE COMPANY,

(LIMITED.)

Incorporated by Act of Parliament. Government Stamped Policies issued. (25 & 26 Vic., cap. 89.)

CHIEF OFFICES:

BRITANNIA BUILDINGS, OXFORD PLACE, LEEDS.

Consolidated Decennial Revenue Account.

In accordance with "The Life Assurance Companies Act, 1870" (33, 34 Vic., ch. 61).

	£	s.	d.		£	s.	d.
Premiums	11,303	15	2	Claims under Policies (after deduction of sums reassured)	3917	4	2
Interest and Dividend	118	13	8	Commission	3056	12	4½
Shareholders' Capital	275	0	0	Expenses of Management	3451	16	11
				Dividend and Bonuses	167	2	6
				Amount of Funds on the 31st July, 1880, the end of the period, as per First Schedule....	1104	12	10½
	£11,697	8	10		£11,697	8	10

Share Capital, £25,000, in 25,000 Shares.

J. P. OGDEN, Sec.   S. ROODHOUSE, Chairman.

THOS. LEADLEY, Vice-Chairman.

Respectable Men wanted as Agents. Apply to the Secretary.

LONDON : Printed by PAGE & PRATT, 5, 6 & 7, Ladgate Circus Buildings, E.C.—May 15 1884.

[REGISTERED FOR]. [TRANSMISSION ABROAD.

THE INSURANCE SPECTATOR OF LONDON

London: Published at 5, Ludgate Circus Buildings, E.C.

ENTERED AT STATIONERS' HALL.] [PUBLISHED SEMI-MONTHLY.

Vol. VI., No. 66. MAY 1st, 1884. Price 4d.

POSITIVE GOVERNMENT SECURITY

LIFE ASSURANCE COMPANY, LIMITED.

HEAD OFFICE:—

34, CANNON STREET,
LONDON, E.C.

MANAGER & ACTUARY:

A. G. MACKENZIE,
F.F.A., A.I.A.

POSITIVE

Those about to ASSURE are requested to examine the System of The POSITIVE, which is unlike any other and is UNEQUALLED for

SIMPLICITY, SECURITY, & LIBERALITY.

The POSITIVE is the ONLY Company in which the Assured can stop payment at any time without a sacrifice.

The POSITIVE is the ONLY Company the Bankruptcy of which would not affect its Policyholders.

MY TABLETS—MEET IT IS, I SET IT DOWN—*Hamlet.*

No. 69.—Vol. VI.   JUNE 16, 1884.   SEMI-MONTHLY 4d.

SCRAPS.

P. T. Barnum says:—Advertise your business. Don't hide your light under a bushel. Whatever your occupation or calling may be, if it needs support from the public, advertise it thoroughly and efficiently, in some shape or other, that will arrest public attention. I freely confess that what success I have had in life may fairly be attributed more to the public press than to nearly all other causes combined. There may possibly be occupations that do not require advertising, but I cannot well conceive what they are.

No, thank you, Tom.

They met, when they were girl and boy,
  Going to school one day,
And " won't you take my peg-top, dear ? "
  Was all that he could say.
She bit her little pinafore,
  Close to his side she came,
She whispered, " No ! no, thank you, Tom,"
  But took it all the same.

They met one day the selfsame way,
  When ten swift years had flown ;
He said, " I've nothing but my heart,
  But this is yours alone."
" And won't you take my heart ? " he said,
  And called her by her name ;
She blushed and said, " No thank you, Tom,"
  But took it all the same.

And twenty, thirty, forty years,
  Have brought them care and joy,
She had the little peg-top still,
  He gave her when a boy.

" I've had more wealth, sweet wife," says he,
  " I've never brought you fame,"
She whispered, " No, no, thank you, Tom,
  You have loved me all the same."

A crusty "Young Benedict" writes:—
" My dear Lorgnette,—The ingenuity and perseverance displayed by some of our insurance companies is indeed marvellous, and the way in which they hunt out those who have not insured their lives or houses is very novel. Some time ago I had the fortune or misfortune—whichever it may be—to enter the connubial state, but no sooner had I registered myself than I was besieged by the agents of four different assurance companies. One would think that the cares and anxieties at such a time are quite sufficient in themselves without being worried with such distracting thoughts as making provision for death. Yet all to no purpose ; these agents called and recalled upon me, and at last getting my better-half to join in the fray, made matters so terribly unbearable that I was glad to give way to one of them, and now I have peace. Should any of my readers have undergone an ordeal similar to mine, I can only say that they have my heartfelt sympathy. The way these agents work is to go to the principal churches, and when the banns are proclaimed they copy down the addresses. Likewise at the registrar's office, when the names appear on the 'board,' they come, and taking down the addresses, immediately set out on the war-path. Should the parties not be at home, they return and return, until such time as they gain admittance. I need scarcely add that the competition is great, and the advantages offered by some of the companies are startling. As much of the success of the companies, however, depends on their agents, one can scarcely wonder at the enormous increase of members within the past year or two when such tactics are adopted."

doting old ladies, who are really affectionate towards them. There's the basis of my company— a vast number of dogs held high in the estimation of the wealthy people. You admit that? Very well, I establish an insurance company. I get in the shape of premiums four or five shillings, or say even 20s. to a dog. Seven years is the average age of a dog and in seven years I collect quite a little premium, don't I?"

"Well?"

"Well! Don't it dawn on you yet. Every time I insure a dog I take his photograph; and what I undertake at his death is to replace the poor departed pet by an exact living counterpart of his old self. In that way I get ahead of the pangs of a separation by death—one of the most poignant of all human sufferings."

"Won't there be any difficulty matching dogs?"

"Not the slightest. Why should there be? All dogs look alike, don't they? Besides, I shall have a large stock to choose from, and I shall match every dog as soon as I get his photograph. Before the dead dog has had time to cool I'll have another in his place, and his pretty mistress will have to rub her eyes twice to make sure she's not dreaming. Of course it will be expensive running the menagerie, but just look at the profits on the premiums. What do you think of it? Think well of it, eh? I thought so. I suppose you wouldn't mind letting me have 20s. as a starter, to be taken out in stock? Haven't got so much? Tuff, by thunder."

The Housekeeper's Tragedy.

One day, as I wandered, I heard a complaining,
 And saw a poor woman, the picture of gloom;
She glared at the mud on her door-step ('twas raining),
 And this was her wail as she wielded her broom:

"Oh! life is a toil, and love is a trouble,
 "And beauty will fade, and riches will flee,
"And pleasures they dwindle, and prices they double,
 "And nothing is what I could wish it to be.

"There's too much of worriment goes to a bonnet;
 "There's too much of ironing goes to a shirt;
"There's nothing that pays for the time you waste on it;
 "There's nothing that lasts us but trouble and dirt.

"In March it is mud; it's slush in December;
 "The midsummer breezes are loaded with dust;
"In fall the leaves litter; in muggy September
 "The wall-paper rots and the candlesticks rust.

"There are worms in the cherries, and slugs in the roses,
 "And ants in the sugar, and mice in the pies.
"The rubbish of spiders no one supposes,
 "And ravaging roaches, and damaging flies.

"It's sweeping at six, and it's dusting at seven;
 "It's victuals at eight, and it's dishes at nine;
"It's potting and panning from ten to eleven;
 "We scarce break our fast ere we plan how to dine.

"With grease and with grime, from corner to centre,
 "For ever at war, and for ever alert,
"No rest for a day, lest the enemy enter—
 "I spend my whole life in a struggle with dirt.

"Last night in my dream, I was stationed for ever
 "On a little bare isle in the midst of the sea;
"My one chance of life was a ceaseless endeavour
 "To sweep off the waves ere they swept off poor me.

"Alas! 'twas no dream—again I behold it!
 "I yield: I am helpless my fate to avert."
She rolled down her sleeves; her apron she folded;
 Then lay down and died, and was buried in dirt.

An **Old-Time Life Insurance Story.** —The late H. H. Hyde, who a generation ago did more than any living man in the United States, at that early day, to make life insurance popular and at the same time lay the foundations of the *Mutual* Life's wonderful prosperity—and whose son, the President of the *Equitable* Life, has since become the most progressive and famous of life managers—is quoted by *Insurance* as telling this story as a part of his experience: He had called many times on a well-to-do merchant, to see if he could not induce him to take out a liberal policy, but all without avail. However, he continued to call, and like a true preacher of life insurance righteousness, too, in season and out of season. It so happened one day he called very much out of season. The merchant's mind was disturbed, he did not wish to be interrupted; he lost his temper, and he lost it to such a degree that he ordered the agent off from his premises. It was a bad job apparently, and no doubt the merchant was grieved at heart over what he had done, his only consolation being in the thought that he was at least rid of an annoyance. How he must have been surprised the very next morning, just as he was sitting down to open his letters, at seeing the imperturbable agent standing at the door, hat in hand! Before he had a chance to recover from his astonishment, his ears were greeted with these words: "I beg your pardon, sir, for again interrupting you, but the truth is I could not get to sleep last night until I had promised myself that I would call once more and remonstrate with you on the course you are pursuing in refusing to protect your business and your family by life insurance." Mr. Hyde was at once invited to come in, the merchant apologized; nay, he did more, for he signed an application then and there for all the insurance the *Mutual* was willing to write on him. In later years, when Mr. Hyde told this story, it had grown. The once prosperous merchant was dead, and he left not a dollar to his family besides his insurance.

"If I place my money in the savings bank," inquired one of the newly arrived, "when can I draw it out again?" "Oh!" responded his Hibernian friend, "sure an' if you put it in to-day, you can get it out to-morrow, by giving a fortnight's notice."

Personals.

Mr. H. H. Friedley, has been appointed a special agent for the *Royal* Insurance Company for the State of Indiana.

Mr. W. Grant, of 181, West George-street, Glasgow, has been appointed inspector of agents for Scotland to the *Crown Life* Assurance Company.

Mr. Edward Litchfield, United States manager of the *Lancashire Insurance* Company, is at present visiting the general agencies of the company in the West.

Mr. W. S. Caine, M.P. for Scarborough, has been elected a director of the *United Kingdom* Temperance and General Provident Institution, *vice* Mr. Samuel Bowly, deceased.

Mr. William Grant, inspector of agencies of the *Scottish* Life Office, has been appointed by the *Crown* Life Assurance Company inspector of agents for Scotland, with offices at 181, West George-street, Glasgow.

Mr. Martin Bennett, jun. United States manager of the *Lion Fire* and the *Scottish Union and National,* is making a Western trip in the interest of his companies. Mr. Bennett will spend some time in California.

Mr. T. W. Letton the western manager of the *Fire Insurance* Association, who has his office in Chicago, has been busy throughout the month in making trips to various parts of his field. Our word for it, the results will be seen in the year's business.

Mr. Wm. C. Mackie.—The *Scottish Equitable Life* Assurance Society are about to open a branch office in Birmingham, at 26, Corporation-street, under the charge of Mr. Wm. C. Mackie, the local manager of the *South British and National* and *Adelaide* Fire Companies. Mr. Mackie, who at one time represented the *Scottish Equitable* in Liverpool, has recently been acting for the *New York Life* Office in the Midland Counties.

TO WHAT EXTENT IS LIFE INSURANCE PROGRESSING?

At the annual meeting of the Institute of Actuaries, the president, Mr. T. B. Sprague, ventured upon the assertion that life insurance in this country is becoming increasingly appreciated, and more commonly practised. Had Mr. Sprague rested this statement upon his own personal knowledge or investigations, there are probably few who would have hesitated to accept it; for in all questions relating to life assurance no one can speak with greater authority than he. It was not, however, on his own observation, but on the statistics adduced by the writer of an essay submitted to the Institute that Mr. Sprague based his expression of opinion, and we are inclined to doubt whether the figures presented really justified the inference drawn from them. Referring to the tables furnished by the writer of the essay, the president is reported to have said:—"The most interesting columns, perhaps, are those relating to the number of policies in force. These have increased from 1,800,000 to 7,200,000, but these figures include a very large number of industrial policies. Excluding them, the ordinary policies have increased [between 1871 and 1883] from 741,000 to 950,000. Mr. Rusher [the writer of the essay] then compares these figures with the population of the country, and finds that the percentage of policies to population has increased from 2¼ per cent. in 1871 to 2⅔ per cent. in 1883."

For various reasons, however, a comparison of the number of life policies in force at different dates is a very unreliable measure of the progress of the business in the interval. To instance only one cause of disturbance, it is obvious that the number of policies will be affected by a high or a low death rate, and is thus subject to fluctuations which have no connection at all with the popularity or unpopularity of the practice of insurance. A very much better test of the progress of the business than that to which Mr. Sprague referred, is to be obtained by a comparison of the amount of the new assurances effected in different years. And in order to admit of such a comparison being made, we have drawn up the following table, which gives, so far as is possible, the amount of new sums assured by the British offices in various years during the past decade. It will be observed that, following Mr. Sprague's example, we have taken no account of the business done by industrial companies.

NEW SUMS ASSURED BY BRITISH COMPANIES.

Name of Company.	1882-3.	1879-80.	1876-7.	1873-4.
	£	£	£	£
Alliance	384,470	340,140	217,200	239,397
Atlas	—	—	—	—
Albion	—	Wound	up	119,850
British Empire	723,319	320,042	265,654	249,256
British Equitable	400,375	407,699	472,091	420,570
Briton	149,124	165,728	233,223	est'b 1875
Briton Med. & Gen.	Ceased to	tr'nsact n	ew busine	ss 352,620
Caledonian	289,289	200,206	257,950	161,099
*Church of England	—	—	—	—
City of Glasgow	361,950	356,810	335,980	376,100
Clergy Mutual	315,525	247,350	326,350	360,410
Cler., Med., & Gen.	357,374	327,694	303,090	341,475
Commercial Union	404,103	324,806	399,961	224,677
Crown	432,650	265,820	256,883	368,175
Colonial	{Absorb'd	by Lond.	} 149,200	198,150
	Ednbrgh	&Glasgw.}		
Eagle	472,430	423,633	215,420	420,000
Economic	274,085	301,645	328,150	334,166
Edinburgh	496,224	511,253	696,937	632,482
Emperor	50,000	51,292	50,225	131,197
Eng. & Scott. Law	231,980	432,935	385,260	491,780
Equitable	155,150	199,150	124,600	147,100
Equity and Law	522,082	366,842	288,195	293,952
Friends Provident	217,172	224,464	192,958	167,100
General	552,830	513,695	452,846	310,725
Gt. Britain Mutual	wind	ing up	284,590	374,302
Gresham	2,138,299	1,935,031	1,852,592	1,533,511
Guardian	313,747	265,800	231,292	217,171
Hand-in-Hand	262,170	251,055	220,730	185,583
*Imperial	—	—	—	—
Lancashire	187,320	say 200000	281,350	187,750
Law Life	347,581	421,000	319,560	285,610
Law Union	216,157	200,696	301,240	207,460
Legal and General	290,000	273,980	250,500	232,390

Name of Company.	1882-3.	1879-80.	1876-7.	1873-4.
	£	£	£	£
Life Assoc. of Scot.	821,552	830,499	881,240	909,922
Lvpl.,Lond.& Globe	503,149	397,202	354,144	409,458
Lond. & Lancashire	544,890	453,687	427,095	281,379
Lond., Edin. & Glas.	127,380	establish	ed 1881.	—
Lond. & Pro. Law { am'l.with Guardian }		128,939	228,299	208,620
London Assurance	263,359	213,063	235,470	340,693
London Life Assoc.	369,600	333,750	349,950	398,400
*Marine & General	—	—	—	—
Masonic & General	(?) 25,000	(?) 30,000	59,660	47,373
Metropolitan	204,426	164,700	231,800	202,450
*Midland Counties	—	—	—	—
Mutual	150,550	125,050	115,960	150,230
*National of Ireland	—	—	—	—
National Life	167,350	297,364	102,226	say 100000
National Provident	320,000	380,300	423,620	316,700
N. Brit. & Mrcntle.	814,819	988,340	1,003,589	672,117
Northern	364,068	535,428	366,310	295,869
Norwich Union	239,310	251,909	338,337	237,600
*Patriotic of Ireland	—	—	—	—
*Pelican	—	—	—	—
Positive	136,770	106,925	86,710	444,755
Provident	575,520	544,841	576,233	274,105
Provident Clerks	292,815	226,846	252,000	203,200
*Provincial	—	—	—	—
Queen	271,830	292,137	192,905	210,379
Reliance	282,040	281,424	458,975	266,135
Rock	188,993	(?)200,000	(?)200,000	229,855
Royal	447,375	499,072	504,519	498,904
*Royal Exchange	—	—	—	—
Sceptre	172,550	141,910	142,695	100,640
Scottish Amicable	508,594	489,762	347,597	427,581
Scottish Equitable	640,519	550,625	506,265	529,340
Scottish Imperial	278,625	228,908	206,000	102,925
Scottish Life	101,497	Estab	lished 18	81.
Scottish Metropltn.	156,605	121,647	106,250	{ Est. 1876. }
Scottish National { Amalgam ated with Scottish Union. }			423,660	448,225
Scottish Provident	1,041,923	1,054,566	1,074,312	1,120,572
Scottish Provincial	240,250	318,148	311,715	351,092
†Scott. Temperance	69,425	Estab	lished 18	83.
Scottish Union (1880 and 1883, Scottish Union & National)	633,116	603,702	410,733	429,710
Scottish Widows	1,289,620	1,569,145	1,276,001	1,152,305
Sovereign	—	144,115	187,863	186,825
Standard	1,487,475	1,436,701	1,334,879	1,088,666
Star	738,057	678,010	684,254	511,241
*Sun	—	—	—	—
Union	269,935	284,926	244,160	290,430
United Kgdm. Tmp.	619,746	587,061	582,512	463,301
Universal	145,493	148,340	220,119	221,767
University	80,050	81,450	74,900	100,800
Western Counties	81,725	203,125	96,150	80,115
West of England	228,205	126,098	235,170	179,355
Westmstr. & Genrl.	99,280	94,157	135,383	111,042
Whittington	155,077	243,382	190,740	184,303
*Yorkshire	—	—	—	—
Total	26,693,969	25,976,020	25,574,427	24,344,518

Here we find that instead of the increment in the amount of the new assurances exceeding the growth of population, it has failed to keep pace with it. Comparing 1873-4 with 1882-3, there is an increase in the new sums assured of 2,349,400, or about 9·6 per cent., which perhaps corresponds pretty closely with the increase of population. But if the period of 1876-7 to 1882-3 be taken, it

---

* These offices have not, during the period dealt with, made public the new business done.

(?) In the few cases so marked returns are not obtainable, and the amounts given are approximations.

† July to December, 1883.

is found that, while in the interval population has risen by about 6¼ per cent., the amount of the new insurances has increased by only £820,000, or about 3⅛ per cent. It must, of course, be remembered that in recent years the business of life insurance—like all other branches of our trade—has had serious difficulties to contend against. Capital has not been reproducing itself to the same extent as it did in previous years of greater prosperity, and many people have not been so well able as they formerly were to make provision against the future. On the other hand, however, the discredit into which many classes of investments have fallen, by causing an accumulation of unused capital might have been expected to benefit to some extent the insurance companies, who undoubtedly offer what, within due limits, is a pre-eminently sound and beneficial form of investment; and it is notorious that the efforts of the companies to get new business have of late years become increasingly keen and pertinacious. With what comparatively small measure of success these efforts have been attended, the table given above sufficiently shows. And while in the circumstances too much should not be made of the slowness in the growth of the business, we fail to see how, in the face of the figures given, it can be maintained that the practice of life insurance is extending more rapidly than can be accounted for by the growth of population. The very opposite appears to be the case, and the business of life insurance, when measured by the increase of population, shows instead of progress a relative retrogression.

This is a state of things which all who are interested in the spread of provident habits must regret to see. And it is all the more to be regretted, because to some extent it is due to preventible cause. There can be no doubt whatever that one reason why life assurance has not attained to that popularity which it deserves is, that the offices have not treated insurers as liberally and equitably as they ought to have done. In what respect they have fallen short of what was to be expected of them we have on various occasions pointed out, and it is not necessary again to enter into details. But, as an instance, take the one question of surrender values. It is only the other day that at a meeting of one of the oldest of the Scottish offices, the chairman took credit to his institution for having adopted the equitable principle of non-forfeiture of surrender values. But what he either failed to know himself or failed to tell his hearers was, that in that very office the great bulk of the policy-holders remain subject to the forfeiture of the surrender value of their policies if they fail to apply for it within thirty days of the lapsing of the policy becoming due. In other words, the money which the chairman acknowledged to belong in equity not to the office, but to the insurers, is appropriated by the former, if the latter fails to put forward an immediate claim to it. It is such one-sided rules as these that militate against the popularity of life insurance, and it is not until they are altered that the business can realise its full measure of success. Happily, it is now being recognised by a good many of the most progressive of the offices, that a number of the conditions of their policies, while they benefit the offices little, are unfair and confusing to insurers, and consequently, restrictive of business. Some considerable reforms have, therefore, been effected of late, and if this more liberal policy is continued and developed, there can be little doubt that life insurance will make a much more rapid advance in the future than it has done hitherto. And we may, perhaps, be permitted to add that we should be all the more sanguine of future success if the purely actuarial element were given somewhat less prominence and power in the direction of the offices. In their own sphere actuaries are, of course, invaluable, and it is upon their investigations and calculations that the whole fabric of insurance rests. But the very fact that they are immersed in mathematical abstractions is calculated to impair their efficiency as men of business. They are not brought sufficiently in contact with the public to know and appreciate their wants, or to discover the best means of satisfying them. They are men of the study rather than of the market place, and as the trade of life insurance, like all other trades, must, if it is to be successful, be conducted on business principles, the active conduct of the affairs of the offices is best entrusted to men who have had a business training, and possess business aptitudes. A study of the table given above will show that, with one or two noteworthy exceptions, which go rather to prove than to contravert the rule, it is the offices that have been conducted on this principle that have achieved the largest measure of success.—*Economist*.

VICARIOUS HEROISM.

THERE is perhaps nothing very blamable, and certainly nothing unnatural, in the serenity with which most men contemplate the possibility of others getting into trouble or undergoing privation or suffering. Each one's burdens are usually heavy enough, and the skeleton in his own closet unquiet enough, to employ his time and faculties and weigh down his mind pretty effectually, without taking the physical or mental loads of others on himself in addition. The famous resolution of Artemus Ward to shed the blood of all his wife's relations sooner than allow the war to fail, and the good old stories of the patriot who " fit, bled, and died for his country " by substitute, and of the absentee Irish landlord who wrote to his agent, " Tell the tenants that no threats to shoot you will terrify me," are typical of certain phases of human nature, not much overcharged. It is true, immediate suffering or pain visibly occurring will often bring forth the most devoted self-sacrifice for rescue or alleviation ; the feelings can often be wrought on even to the overcoming of the judgment. The scene in " Dred," where the legislator who has just helped pass a stringent fugitive-slave law takes a long night-ride through mud and storm to aid a fugitive slave in escaping, is familiar to everyone. But when sacrifice is

demanded in order to prevent possible suffering to others which by its very nature cannot possibly touch one's self, and which *may* not happen at all, it takes a hard struggle with the inertia and the selfishness of average human nature to make the exertion and incur the outlay.

Nevertheless, there is one class of cases where every sentiment of honour, good faith, and affection combined should (but too often do not) operate to overcome this sluggishness and carelessness ; namely, those where the parties on whom the chance blow may fall are one's own wife and children. Here it is impossible for any man worth the name to disconnect himself from their sorrows or privations, or to consider them matters of indifference to him even after his own death ; if he has a spark of manhood or even common humanity in him, the *certain* knowledge that they would suffer from cold or hunger or killing drudgery, or even from a lack of those minor comforts and social pleasures which make up so large a part of the comfort of living, would poison his whole term of existence, and cover him with a pall of gloom and wretchedness during all his waking hours. He would leave no stone unturned, spare no effort of body or mind, grudge no outlay or sacrifice to falsify the prophecy and reverse the decree of fate. Even if affection failed to stimulate him, honour would reinforce it ; he has tied that woman to his service and burdened her with helpless children, he has brought these children into the world to be conscious of misery, and he has no right—if he stops to think of it, he *knows* he has no right—to regard his duty as ended when he has shared his wages with them, and given them equal portion with himself of such food and clothing and furniture and reading matter and entertainments as those wages will purchase from month to month. The duty he owes to them extends far beyond that he owes to himself, but if *he* ceases from earthly labour, he ceases also from earthly needs and consciousness and suffering, and his power of satisfying his wants is likely to cease only *with* those wants ; while such cessation on his part leaves his family with requirements no smaller than before, but robbed at a blow of the whole means of satisfying them, and exposed to a destitution alleviated only by the cold and scanty dole of charity, the precarious and occasional help of friends, or by an unceasing drudgery which makes life scarcely worth the keeping. So to leave them is the grossest of bad faith : it is a violation of the promise of protection given at marriage, and implied in the very nature of the contract, for it leaves the woman far more helpless than she would have been if he had never married her.

What, then, is the reason that so many men act as though these considerations had no weight with them ? Evidently, it is in large measure because instead of dealing with certainties, they relate only to contingencies. It is because men can cheat themselves into the belief that in the great lottery of premature death, *their* names will be left off the roll ; that the bullets which are striking down their companions all around them will leave *them* unarmed ; that in a world swarming with murderous accidents *they* will never meet one, and amid thronging diseases *they* will be invulnerable; that *their* wives could not possibly ever swell the number of haggard and half-starved widows who wear out their lives in a struggle for bare existence, and *their* children cannot be among the ragged and ignorant gamins who recruit at best the ranks of unskilled labourers labouring precariously at starvation wages, and perhaps those of the outlaws of society. Yet we know that ignoring or defying the facts of life will not change them, and that no exception will be made in favour of the careless, the contumacious, or the stupid. Any given family is as likely as any other given one, ordinarily speaking, to be pauperised by the unexpected death of the wage-earner; and there is but one way for him to make sure that such shall not be the result. He cannot prevent death, but he can prevent its finding him penniless. He cannot rely for this on savings, which will cease at his death; but he can for a small sum procure a responsible company to guarantee his family a sum sufficient to swell what they can easily earn into a comfortable maintenance, to keep the colour in the wife's cheeks and the light in her eyes, and give the children a fair education and a trade or a start in a clerkship or profession.

The man who refuses to take this fair and obvious precaution is simply playing hero by proxy, like the ones we cited above. He is sending his wife and children to war as substitutes for himself. He is not taking any risk: he is making them take one, and one which he is bound by every consideration of honour and love to protect them from. He is giving himself—them too, doubtless, but that does not mend matters any—a little more money to spend, a few more of the luxuries of life at present, and paying for them with the money which should go to form a fund for their support when he can no longer support them. He has no right to that money: it belongs to them. His action is not heroic or spirited or praiseworthy in any way: it is simply a barbarian's heedless and gluttonous sacrifice of the future to the present, only in this case of other people's future; and that those others too often urge him to that disregard, and plant thorns in the way of his providing for their welfare, does not excuse him,—it is his business to overrule their prejudice or thoughtlessness, and act wisely on their behalf, even if they do not appreciate it till circumstances vindicate his course.

"Pat" said his reverence, "I shall be very busy this afternoon, and if anyone calls I do not wish to be disturbed." "All right, sor; will I tell them you're not in?" "No, Pat; that would be a lie." "An phwat'll I say, yer riverence?" "Oh, just put them off with an evasive answer." At supper time Pat was asked if anyone had called. "Fax, there did." "And what did you tell him?" said the priest. "Shure, an' I gave an evasive answer. He axed me was yer honor in, an' I sez to him, sez I, 'Was yer gran'mother a hoot-owl?'"

THE ACTUARY, No. 39.

Mr. John Graunt, F.R.S.
(Continued from page 187.)

MANY subsequent writers have betrayed more fear of the punishment they might be liable to on making similar disclosures, and have kept entirely out of sight the sources of their conclusions. The immunity they have thus purchased from contradiction could not be obtained but at the expense of confidence in their results.—*Lubbock and Drinkwater* (p. 44).

Mr. E. J. Farren (*Life Contingencies*, p. 17), says:—

"The circumstance of the plague occurring during the earlier years of Graunt's publication may, in part, account for the rather extraordinary demand for the work—probably as a matter of curiosity as to the Bills of Mortality it contained—for the Great Fire of London happening in 1666, the year following the fourth edition, and by extensive devastation rendering the city less crowded with buildings, the plague finally disappeared, and ten years elapsed before a new edition of Graunt's Treatise was called for."

Charles II. recommended the Royal Society to elect Graunt one of its members, charging the Fellows of the Society, "That if they found any more such tradesmen, they should admit them all;" and Graunt attributed the absence of the plague during the year 1660 to the circumstances of the restoration of his Royal Patron!

Yet, notwithstanding all this, some doubts have been raised as to whether Graunt really was the author of this work at all—whether in fact the real author were not Sir Wm. Petty. We have taken some pains to investigate this charge, and have come to the conclusion that it is founded in error. The misconception probably arose in the circumstance that Sir Wm. Petty—who was a relative of Graunt's—often spoke of the edition which he edited after Graunt's death as his own.

Then again, Bishop Burnet, in his "History of his Own Times," casually alludes to Sir Wm. Petty as the real author, and so fans the flame of doubt. Evelyn and Halley both supported the side of Sir Wm. Petty, as Mr. Hodge, F.I.A., has done at a later date (vide *Assurance Magazine*, vol. viii., p. 234). Anthony Wood says the observations were done upon certain hints and advice of Sir Wm. Petty.

In support of the absolute authorship by Graunt there is the following testimony :—Dr. Sprat, the historian of the Royal Society, and also a contemporary, ascribes, without hesitation or qualification of any kind, the work to Graunt. Sir Wm. Petty, in a letter to his intimate friend, Sir Wm. Southwell, five years after Graunt's death, and when he had no motive for disguise or concealment (if he ever had any), refers to the work as Graunt's, without any insinuation direct or indirect respecting its paternity. McCulloch (referring to the authorities on the other side) says:—" Notwithstanding the deference due to their authority, it may be doubted whether there be any good ground for this statement." To which we devoutly say, Amen.

While the book remained so popular, its author fell speedily into disgrace. Graunt was a Roman Catholic, and also a director of the New River Company ; and he was accused of having, in his latter capacity, intercepted the supply of water during the Great Fire of London—his religious views leading him to support the conspiracy, in which so many persons, who might have known better, then believed. He survived the foolish charge, although through it, as Mr. Hodge has pointed out, his name has become associated with both life and fire insurance. He was further charged with not having returned some of the early Bills of Mortality lent to him by the Company of Parish Clerks for the purpose of preparing his book.

There is also ascribed to Graunt:—" Reflections on the Bills of Mortality relative to the Plague, 1665." And it is further said he left some MS. writings.

In view of some of the preceding statements, we think it well to add the entire passage from Burnet's " History of his Own Times," wherein, writing of the Fire of 1666, and the incidents associated with it —more particularly in regard to its having been designedly occasioned by the Papists—he says (edition 1850, p. 156):—

" There was one Graunt, a papist, under whose name Sir Wm. Petty published his ' Observations on the Bills of Mortality ;' he had some time before applied himself to Lloyd, who had great credit with the Countess of Clarendon ; and said he could raise that estate the [New River Company] considerably if she would make him a trustee for her. His schemes were probable; and

he was made one of the board that governed that matter : and by that he had a right to come as often as he pleased to view their works at Islington. He went thither on Saturday before the fire broke out, and called for the key of the place where the heads of the pipes were, and turned all the cocks that where then open, and stopped the water, and went away, and carried the keys with him. So when the fire broke out next morning, they opened the pipes in the streets to find water, but there was none. And some hours were lost in sending to Islington, where the door was to be broken open and the cocks turned. And it was long before the water got to London. Graunt indeed denied that he had turned the cocks. But the officer of the works affirmed that he had, according to order, set them all running, and that no person had got the keys from him besides Graunt ; who confessed he had carried away the keys, but pretended he did it without design."

Graunt died in 1674.—*Insurance Cyclopædia.*

CORRESPONDENCE.

THE ATLAS INSURANCE COMPANY.

To the Editor.

SIR,—My attention has just been called to some remarks in your issue of the 16th instant, with respect to my notice of motion relative to admitting Press representatives to the annual general meetings of the Atlas Insurance Company, in which I am a shareholder. The question is a simple one, and my object is quite specifically enough stated in the terms of the motion itself. However, I would thank you for allowing me to say that I am moving in this matter neither as a lawyer nor in any biassed spirit of antagonism to the direction or to its secretary (Mr. S. J. Pipkin), with whom I stand on perfectly good terms. Being both a shareholder and policy-holder, I have certainly a natural inducement in directing myself to a principle which I would like to see carried out in all our insurance as in all our other companies, and especially now that the American and other companies are running us so close in the matter of competition. My holding, too, I may mention, in reply to your remark, is sufficiently large to give me three votes. As to my motion, a "call for a change"—which you yourselves consider at least partly desirable, can only be brought about, I think, by someone coming forward in the way I humbly intend to do, as well in my own as in the general interest.

Yours obediently,

CHARLES HANCOCK,

Temple, E.C., *Tuesday, June 25th,* 1884.

TERMS OF SUBSCRIPTION.

ANNUAL Subscription (including postage), Paid in advance, 9s.

NOTICE TO CORRESPONDENTS.

All Communications intended for insertion to be addressed to the Editor, " The INSURANCE SPECTATOR OF LONDON," 5, Ludgate Circus Buildings, E.C.

THEATRES, &c.

Adelphi Theatre (Strand), "In the Ranks," 8; Alhambra (Leicester-square), "The Beggar Student," 7.45; Criterion (Piccadilly), "Featherbrain," 9; Empire (Leicester-square), "Chilperic," 7.45; Globe (Newcastle street), "The Private Secretary," 8; Lyceum (Strand), "Much Ado About Nothing," 8; Novelty (Great Queen-street), "Nita's First," 8; Princess's (Oxford-street), "Claudian," 8; Prince's (Piccadilly), "Called Back," 9; Vaudeville (Strand), "Confusion," 9; Royal Aquarium Promenade Concerts, 8; Maccabe's Entertainment, St. James's Hall, 8; Maskelyne and Cooke (Egyptian Hall), 8.

CONTENTS :

THE

Insurance Spectator of London.

JULY 1, 1884.

THERE are two schemes about which we should like to know something. One is the *Provident Association of England, Limited*, and the other is the *John Bull* Insurance Company, Limited. If Mr.

E. D. Greenwood will enlighten us as to the history of the former, and our old friend Mr. Harold inform us as to the financial position of the latter, the communications shall appear without charge. Recent legal proceedings render the previous procedure of the *Provident Association of England* matter of interest, and enquiries concerning Mr. Harold and the *John Bull* are now becoming frequent enough to be significant.

IN another column we allow the *Economist* to utter its snarl against the administration of life insurance in this country. If the writer of the article in question had been conversant with the subject upon which he presumed to write, he would have known that life offices, of late years, have vied with each other in affording facilities to insurers. We are willing to admit that the growth of life insurance is not on a level with the increase of the population, or the requirements of the community, but, in our view, the reason is a very different one to that given by the *Economist*. We have always felt that a mistake was committed when Parliament enacted that no new life office should be registered until £20,000 had been deposited. It is a phase of *protection*, and has not worked well. It was not so much the *number* of life offices which caused mischief, as the secrecy in regard to accounts. In the latter respect the Act has done good, but in practically eliminating the element of competition it has worked evil.

THOSE employers who have contracted themselves out of the Employers' Liability Act and made terms with their workmen may study with profit a decision given by Mr. Justice Butt at the Yorkshire Assizes. Last year Mr. Radcliffe, an engineer and contractor, of Sheffield, took out a policy of assurance with the *Ocean, Railway, and General Accident* Assurance Company in respect to any accident to any of his workmen. Among other matters, the policy set forth that the Company would pay compensation to the assured, should any of his workpeople sustain bodily injuries, or in the event of accidents other than those for which he might be liable under the Employers' Liability Act. In November a workman was killed by accident at Mr. Radcliffe's works, and, after some correspondence, the Company contended that they were not called upon to pay compensation, inasmuch as Mr.

Radcliffe was not liable for the accident either under the Employers' Liability Act or at common law. Mr. Justice Butt has decided in favour of the Company. The assured, therefore, has recovered nothing. Had Mr. Radcliffe been liable under the Act, the Company would doubtless have paid. But the case is a curious illustration of what may happen when employers, anxious to be outside the purview of the Employers' Liability Act, assure themselves against accidents for which they may or may not be liable.

THE following return, extracted from the reports of the Fire Insurance Companies so far made public for the year 1883, will be found useful. It is interesting to notice that the large companies have, as a rule, done better in 1883 than in 1882. All the offices, for instance, having a premium income exceeding £400,000 show a diminished loss rate. This is perhaps accounted for by the greater power of these companies to eliminate unsound business, and to exact adequate premium rates. Their averages are likewise probably better, because larger. Several important companies, including the *Northern* and the *Royal*, are not included in this table, because their reports have not yet appeared. Three others—the *Phœnix*, the *Sun*, and the *Norwich Union*—never publish any accounts at all.

	Fire Premiums 1883.	Fire Losses 1883.	Percentage of Losses, 1883.	Increase or Decrease of Losses as compared with 1882.	Percentage of Commission and other Expenses.
Law Union	£40,111	£18,922	47.0	same	30.0
Law Fire	104,467	47,939	46.0	+19.3	27.0
City of London	298,862	193,190	64.8	— 8.4	31.7
Scottish Provincial	42,373	24,260	57.3	+ 1.5	28.2
Alliance	312,960	152,186	48.5	+ 1.1	30.3
Yorkshire	62,848	36,653	58.3	+ 2.6	25.4
National	21,305	8,767	41.1	—96.6	48.0
County	211,240	80,191	37.9	—13.1	27.9
Fire Insurance Association ...	244,129	180,542	74.0	+ 9.5	34.5
London Assurance	316,259	205,355	64.9	+ 3.9	31.4
Atlas	95,908	79,623	83.0	+16.3	26.2
Scottish Union and National	202,592	142,970	70.5	+10.5	27.4
Royal Farmers	36,851	24,529	66.0	+18.8	31.0
West of England	97,171	56,614	58.0	—13.0	30.0
Union	59,532	42,458	71.3	+38.2	34.7
Caledonian	93,126	52,332	56.1	— 7.7	33.0
Liverpool, London, and Globe	1,271,478	696,091	54.7	— 9.4	28.9
North British and Mercantile	1,107,745	672,826	60.0	— 2.4	31.0
General	77,755	48,518	62.5	— 3.9	41.0
Lancashire	591,343	420,484	71.0	— 2.6	37.7
Commercial Union	746,091	494,746	66.3	—11.5	39.7
Imperial	791,128	490,428	62.0	— 4.0	28.7
Lion.........................	144,830	96,454	67.9	—13.5	34.4
Guardian	376,834	227,896	60.3	—14.9	29.0
London and Lancashire ...	499,000	324,987	65.1	— 4.9	31.2
Queen	589,810	409,614	69.5	— 9.2	30.0
Manchester	214,931	134,140	62.4	—19.0	29.0
National (of Ireland)	128,177	84,908	66.2	—15.8	26.6
London and Provincial ...	187,773	130,791	69.0	+24.0	40.0
Equitable	45,655	41,064	89.0	— 6.9	25.8
Hand-in-Hand	53,129	33,160	62.4	— 5.4	27.1
Phœnix	}				
Sun	}	Do not publish any accounts.			
Norwich Union	}				

Crumbs.

THE *Insurance Exchange*, Chicago, has been regularly incorporated.

THE name of the last Russian company organised is the *Russ* Fire Insurance Company of St. Petersburg.

THE *Commercial Union* has removed its New York office to its new building, corner of Pine and William Streets.

THE *New York Life* has purchased a site in Berlin, Prussia, and will erect an office building in that city for its German head-quarters.

AT the death of Queen Elizabeth, the peers of England numbered about sixty, and forty of the then existing peerages are now extinct.

THE London offices of the *British Re-insurance* Company, Limited, have been removed to 1, St. Michael's Alley, Cornhill, E.C.

THE SEXES IN PORTUGAL AND GREECE.—In Portugal there are 1,084 females to every 1,000 male inhabitants, while in Greece there are 1,000 men to every 906 women.

THE widow of the late Captain Webb, who lost his life in the Niagara Rapids, is now acting as cashier at the Whirlpool Rapids Park, close by the scene of her husband's fatal plunge.

THE directors of the *British and Foreign Marine* Insurance Company (Limited) have decided to pay an interim dividend of 8s. per share for the half-year ending June 30, 1884, free of income-tax.

AN inquirer asks, " How can I tell classical music?" That is easy enough. When you hear everybody applaud and look relieved after the piece is finished, then you can know it is strictly classical.

IT is getting quite fashionable for wives to murder their husbands for the insurance; but a curious feature is that this occurs solely in regions where divorce is hard to get. Is there any connection?

A FRENCH doctor, not Anti-Jennerian, calls attention to the fact that for many months the death returns from small-pox in Paris, where vaccination is not compulsory, have ranged from one to five weekly, and this week there has not been a single death.

AT the beginning of the fifteenth century a sack of coals cost threepence. At the same period the hire of a horse from Canterbury to London was two shillings and four pence; dinner and supper in the metropolis cost eightpence, and a bed in London for seven nights sevenpence.

THE force of habit is well illustrated in Morgan, the celebrated calculator of lives. A gentleman speaking of having lost so many friends (mentioning the number) in a certain space of time, Morgan coolly took down a book from his shelf, and running his finger down one of the columns of figures, said, " So you ought, sir, and three more."

THE "DO" AND "DON'T" OF CANVASSING.

Do be civil,—Without civility all else is utterly futile. Like the vessel, possessed of every requisite for the voyage, but awaiting the favourable wind; like the landscape, decked with flowers of every hue, exhaling their odours to the summer breeze, filled with trees of all sorts and sizes, but lacking the bright completion of the whole, the glorious sun. " Civility " may frequently seem thrown away, but rest assured it will sooner or later bring its reward. Let two agents representing the same office canvass the same individual for the first time, and, though he may never have thought of assuring his life, he cannot avoid listening to the pleadings of the one, nor can he decline to consider the matter; whereas, the other may, by his want of civility, furnish the very handle sought, an excuse for putting the matter off.

Do be neat. Neatness is a very desirable acquisition of a life assurance canvasser. Neatness in dress, as distinct from " swelldom " or " foppishness " on the one hand, or carelessness on the other. Let there be nothing conspicuous about the attire, nothing in any way calculated to draw off the attention of your client from the subject you are discussing. Neatness, too, in your office arrangements is very desirable, keeping the same object in view, the fixing of the entire attention upon the all-important matter in hand.

Do be courteous.—This may be termed the refinement of civility, and is invaluable to the life agent. The grace will convert the most inveterate foe into your most confirmed friend. This acquirement (for it may be acquired) will compel the careless to afford you a hearing; and when once this is obtained, the good agent knows how to improve it. A friend of ours, who is one of the most successful and intelligent agents it has ever been our pleasure to know, has a very elegantly fitted-up office, situated in a most eligible situation, but the entrance is somewhat marred by an awkward step, formed in a dark and unusual position. Now our friend has by his courtesy made this obstacle a lever for favourably impressing his clients, so that the last thought uppermost in the mind of any who visit him is a strong conviction that H—— is very attentive and obliging—even coming to the door to tell us to " take care of that step, please."

Do be energetic.—We know agents who, by throwing a little more energy into their efforts, would accomplish double the amount of business they now rest satisfied with. Indeed, it is only the one or two " energetic " agents that are known as agents. We recommend energy of style as well as energy of movement. A listless, undecided mode of address will secure small results, whereas an energetic manner arrests and commands attention and even admiration. Apart from the substantial benefits obtained by energetic canvassing, there is the recommendation it naturally conveys to the onlooker—who, the proverb says, " sees most of the game "—both of the company and of the agent. For it requires very superficial observation to connect a busy, active agent with the idea of an "energetic" pushing company, and *vice versâ*.

Do be persevering.—We remember hearing a representative of a very flourishing life office say he had just obtained a "proposal" from a gentleman whom he had canvassed for seven years, and, on asking what it was that enabled him at last to convince the man, he replied, "I ventured to improve the sudden death of an uninsured brother." Yes, sooner or later, perseverance must have its reward. Not spasmodic effort, followed by a lull, but regular systematic canvassing—this alone will bring the full fruition of the agent's toil. It is requisite, however, to intimate here that we advise discriminating perseverance. We know agents who call on more people in one day than they ought to see in a week. On the average we are inclined to think that one in every four individuals will, if wisely canvassed, assure at once; and we would suggest (from experience) that not more than four lives be canvassed each day, sufficient time being devoted to each to see whether it is worth while repeating the visit, or what mode will be the best to adopt on the next occasion. This brings us to the next requisite:

Do be intelligent.—We take it that there is no occupation where it is so requisite to study character as that of canvassing for life assurance. For instance, is the life you call upon older than yourself? Then it won't do to lecture him. Is he younger? Then strive to touch the chords that awaken those sympathies peculiar to his years, and gradually invite him to ponder the line of argument which induced you to see the advantage of life assurance. Is he rich? Respectfully suggest the possibility of an unavoidable loss, and, if not, that life assurance is a good investment. Is he poor? Show him how much a small weekly payment immediately secures. In a word, think, read, meditate, study, converse on this subject of life assurance until you shall be in a position, whenever called upon, to meet every objection, and to plead your cause in an intelligent perspicuous mode. Under this head we may acknowledge the great advantages to be derived from the study of such books as "A Handy Book for Life Assurance Agents," by H. R. Sharman; "The Insurance Guide and Hand-Book," by C. Walford.

Don't be discouraged.—A gentleman of great ability, gave us on one occasion the following remarkable leaf out of his experience:—"For three months I had not taken a single proposal, and was beginning to be discouraged, when, taking advantage of the fact that the next week was the one immediately preceding the general meeting, and offered peculiar advantages to assurers, I took nineteen proposals." And so it is. We find but one experience in this matter; that just when hope is about to give way to despair, the clouds break, the wheel of fortune takes a more cheery turn. While this is the case, however, we cannot estimate too highly—as a means of preventing discouragement—the magical effect of a bright, sanguine countenance. No melancholy man would make a good life assurance agent. It is as

remarkable as it is true, that this matter—so intimately associated with the darkest shades of our lives—can only be successfully effected by a cheerful, pleasant, and agreeable manner.

Do be apt with the rejoinder.—An agent about to take his first appointment informed us that he intended to "jot down a few lines of argument" before he set to work. As well might a schoolboy attempt to gain the ear of the House of Commons. No; it is only by being prepared with an immediate reply suitable to the moment, or a "rejoinder" when some fancied objection is urged, that we can hope to overcome. We have found it beneficial to rehearse in retrospection the whole line of argument in each individual case if we have failed, to enable us to discover the weak points; if we have succeeded, to find out how, next time, it can be done more effectually or more speedily.

Don't be easily put back.—We shall not be far wrong if we state that there was a time in the earlier career of every agent, no matter how successful his after life, when he felt that he received nothing but rebuffs. At first it may appear that there is no other course open than to accept the "decisive reply" and leave; but a very little experience will soon show that it is by no means desirable to accept the verdict so readily pronounced. We heard of an agent being stopped the other day in a secluded village by a client, who wished "to thank him for making him assure." Very frequently it is not until the agent has accepted rebuke after rebuke, repulse followed by repulse, that he can make any impression favourable to his cause. To be "easily put back" is to be false to our colours, to concede that our mission is a trifling one; but to urge day after day, week after week, month after month, year after year, to suggest when sickness has just reminded of the chances of life, when an uninsured friend has left a widow unprovided for, this is to exalt our daily work into its proper place, for life assurance was not inappropriately described by a French writer as "A second Providence."

Don't take No for an answer.—It is difficult, we admit, to learn to act up to this rule, but no more difficult than necessary. The very manner in which the agent will have occasionally to approach his clients suggests the simple, "When I can afford." For instance, we have heard of a gentleman who adopted the following plan for "opening up fresh ground." He took from the daily paper the names and addresses of those who had "increased their olive-branches," those who had "entered into the holy bonds of matrimony," and those who had lost friends. With this list he called on the first-named, and pointed out to them the desirability of making some or further provision for increased responsibilities; to the second class he urged the necessity of placing "something certain" in the event of early death, and with the last class he brought home the lessons taught by the loss of relations as a reminder that preparation against what must occur could only be surely made by life assurance. Now, while this plan continually influenced business, it necessitated the employment not only of great tact but frequent visits. Often, very often, he was offered " No," for an answer, but just as often he tacitly declined to take it, and need we say his patience was rewarded.

Don't be afraid to try again.—If there be one experience more common to all agents than another, it is this, that it was the frequent asking that brought the bulk of their business. Had they hung back from repeating a visit that at first promised little or no result, they would not now count amongst their assured some of their best lives. One morning a very intimate friend of ours was coming down to business in a very depressed frame of mind, owing to the fact of his not having " taken a proposal " for three weeks. He called for the last time on a "life" he had canvassed over and over again. " Well, Mr. ——, I suppose you won't do anything ?" " Well, I don't know." Agent (encouraged), " Shall I take a proposal ?" " Yes, I think you may for £500 at all events." " And when will you see the doctor ?" " Oh, there is no time like the present; suppose we go now together ?" Never will our friend require again to seek in vain for encouragement when "business is slack." The recollection of this timely " take " will ever serve to remind him that it is by no means desirable to " be afraid to try again."

Don't be provoked at indifference.—Recollect the old French proverb, *Chacun à son gout*, and let it remind you we each have our hobby, that after all there will be some who cannot see the benefit or advantage of assuring their lives. Remember, too, that if you appear annoyed at non-success, it may prevent you reaping the benefits which may result from a change of mind, when you certainly will feel " provoked " at being passed by.

THE OLD, OLD STORY.

To the Editor.

SEEING that others have written you concerning their insurance experiences, I will venture to relate those of our family, in the hope that others will profit by the reflections which may be aroused by the reading.

My husband died about ten years ago, leaving me with a son and a daughter and with means sufficient to give them a comfortable start in life, but not sufficient to render them independent during my life-time, therefore I considered it my duty to give them such educations as would enable them to earn their own livings in case any emergency should make it necessary.

My daughter was married about three years ago to a young friend of my son, a merchant, with sufficient money for the purposes of his business, but with nothing over for outside investments. As the business was of such a nature as to make it desirable that some one connected with it should take journeys to the western provinces, and voyages to America, my son-in-law induced my son to join him, and, with the consent of my trustees, I advanced them funds to enable them to carry on their business without being embarassed by the peculiarities or despotisms of bank managers, who so often lead young merchants to make invest-

ments beyond their means, then suddenly withdraw their advances, and so ruin their clients.*

All went well with my two boys, that is, as well as could reasonably be expected, as, of course, they had the usual experiences of bad debts and insolvent customers, but always came out with a sufficient margin of net profit to encourage them, without making sufficient to cause them to be speculative ; so you will readily understand why my son-in-law felt it necessary to live pretty closely in order to provide against any of the calamities which are so apt to befall business men in these times. This prevented him from being popular in our city, where young men and old are esteemed in proportion to the money they spend, regardless of any consideration as to whether the money is their own or not; so that, for the sake of being in " society," many young men are tempted to become members of clubs where gambling is done, and to make other experiments and expenditures, whether they can afford any of them or not, by reason of which many of them acquire habits which involve them in financial and moral ruin.

During the past summer my boys were alarmed by the crop reports, and so did not attempt to increase their business, but rather to confine themselves to their older and most certain customers ; consequently, they imported very few goods for their fall trade, and so ran pretty nearly out of goods by the time their summer shipments were over ; but their collections were very good, and they felt like selecting such goods for the spring trade as would secure them customers who would be sure to pay in any event of general financial prosperity or adversity.

My son-in-law, therefore, left for America in August, although it was very early yet. Having no particular anxieties at home, he thought it would be best to take plenty of time in making his selections and make good bargains ; he wrote from time to time as to his progress and the prospects of purchases, stating at the same time that he would not ship anything until he was about to return, as he thought he could make better terms for freight and passage, if he brought his goods along with himself in the same vessel, and could then look after all the bills of lading and custom duties, so saving expenses of various kinds.

Early in November he wrote that he had everything nearly ready for starting and would leave for home in a few days, also that he believed he had been very successful in his selections and purchases; so my daughter began to count the days of her husband's return, and my son began to build little castles in Spain to make the time pass away for her, sometimes teasing and joking her about her husband's rather long absence, and sometimes consulting with her about a little entertainment he intended to give when he arrived.

---

* Our fair correspondent has evidently fallen into a common error regarding the conservative policy of bankers, which makes itself felt only in periods when too much capital has become absorbed in over-speculation, importation, or production.

We were not certain as to the name of the vessel on which my son-in-law intended to sail, and so did not feel more than the usual anxieties when November passed over without our seeing him, although we saw an account of the loss at sea of a vessel in which he *might* have been on board; yet when December came in without tidings of him, my son cabled across to one of the firms from whom he had bought goods, asking them for information concerning his partner; in a few days he got a reply which threw us all into despair, as it led us to believe that our dear one had taken passage in the ill-fated vessel, and that he was lost to us in this world, and our worst fears were confirmed by the continued silence.

The result of much correspondence between my son and the American merchants with whom he learned that my son-in-law had had dealings, was that he had bought largely and had shipped the goods on the same vessel as he had taken passage for himself, so although, of course, the loss of the goods was nothing in comparison to the loss of the husband of my daughter, whom we all loved and esteemed for his own sake, yet it meant present ruin to all of us, and so added to our misery.

You may be sure that it was with very heavy hearts we parted with my son, who determined to go to America for the purpose of making the best arrangements possible with the creditors of the firm, especially as he was not sure as to all of them, because my son-in-law had with him in the lost vessel the invoices and bills of lading, and had accepted the drafts for the goods purchased, so that it might be some months before, by the ordinary process of presentation of acceptances, he could learn the extent of the responsibilities of the firm, it being also necessary to learn of all in order to make arrangements with all without giving undue preferences to any.

Our second parting left us, two helpless women, with my daughter's young child, fearing every shadow, and sound, and every silence; so we were sick in body and in mind long before we heard of my son's arrival in New York, from which port he sent us a cablegram to the effect that things might not all be as bad as we had dreaded. In about ten days or so we received a letter from him stating that he found and had had an interview with the manager of the bank with whom my son-in-law had done his business before his departure, and through him had reason to believe that the goods had been insured in some of the offices there, but that he had not yet the particulars or any certainty. In a few days more, however, we received another letter stating not only that my son-in-law had obtained marine insurance on the goods, but that he had been induced to take out an accident policy on his own life for the benefit of the firm. Through the insurance companies my son learned the most of the particulars of the shipments, and was enabled to arrange the affairs of the firm by transferring to the creditors the policies of marine insurance, and to duplicate the orders, at the same time collecting the amount of the accident policy, which was for one thousand pounds sterling.

During my son's absence many of the friends and acquaintances of my son-in-law called on us, and many of them inquired if he had not any life insurance; as both myself and my daughter had always spoken strongly against life insurance, and as my son-in-law, after arguing with us until he saw we *would not* be convinced, had ceased to discuss the matter, we were sure he had been overcome by our arguments or talk against it; we were, therefore, very much surprised when the agent of the —— Life Assurance Company called upon my daughter to ask her to sign some papers which he said were to make claim for two thousand pounds as the amount of a policy which my son-in-law had taken out for her benefit.

We have just now learned that my son has landed safely after his return voyage from America, so, although time can ne'er restore to us the dear one we have lost, yet, if possible, his memory is more dear to us by reason of the forethought of his love which caused him to provide insurances in order that his wife and child and partner and myself might not be ruined by any calamity against which he could provide. We feel sure that the moments, few or many, in which he had to prepare for his death were sweetened by the thought of having provided for those so dear to him, instead of being embittered by the reflection that his economies or his extravagances had prevented him from being able or willing to do so.

We cannot be expected to spend a happy year, as we are bereaved of our loved one; yet we are, of course, thankful that his love smoothed the way which would have been very rugged indeed.

I do not know whether you will make a sermon to young men out of this letter, but I think that all of them would be more likely to be happy during the coming years if they were to think of their duties a little more and of their amusements a little less, and were brave enough to avoid the clubs and such like causes of extravagance and debt. You may be sure we have now ideas of insurance very different from those we formerly held, and that for all the managers of all the companies, whether Marine, Accident, or Life, we have only good wishes.

LAW INTELLIGENCE.

HIGH COURT OF JUSTICE, CHANCERY DIVISION.

Before Mr. Justice Pearson.

RE CYCLIST ASSURANCE COMPANY.

This was an application, *ex parte*, for the appointment of a provisional liquidator of this company. It appeared that the company had several thousand agents in England, Scotland, and Ireland, and they were constantly remitting money to the head office. There had been a petition presented for the winding-up of this company, and it was necessary that a provisional liquidator should be appointed to take care of the assets. He asked that the general manager of the company, Mr. Clark, should be appointed provisional liquidator without salary and without security. The Court was further asked to restrain the proceedings in 11 actions against the company pending the hearing of the petition.

Mr. Yett Lee appeared to support the application.

His Lordship appointed Mr. Clark provisional liquidator, and also stayed the proceedings in the actions.

BRITISH FIRE INSURANCE IN THE UNITED STATES.

It has become so much the fashion among a certain class of writers to assume that British underwriters know all about the business of fire insurance and that whatever dangers there may be lying in wait for it the British managers are sure to pilot their companies through them safely, that it seems pretty nearly treason to hint that this may be a mistake. Nevertheless we are going to suggest some reasons for the opinion that our cousins over the water have not yet thoroughly comprehended the business of fire insurance in the United States.

From about the middle of 1879 to the middle of 1882, a period of three years, nine British companies entered this country for business, not including the reinsurance company. These years covered the period of greatest depression in rates and also of excessive losses. The companies came here to get business, and they found plenty of it at current rates. If there was any feeling of conservatism on the part of their American managers about writing freely it was overcome by the pressure from the home officers for more business. Rates, meantime, were going down, very perceptibly to those who watched the growth of term business, but almost imperceptibly to those who, in the words of the *Finance Chronicle*, fail to " take true account of that terrible factor, the unexpired risk."

It has, however, been understood for some time that the American managers, who formerly could not be pushed far enough and fast enough, have been told to halt in their career. The figures of last year's business show this clearly even if we had not the positive assurance of the fact from the official utterances of managers and chairmen at annual meetings on the other side. They are not so anxious for American business. The unexpired risk has caught them in its clutches and there is but one of two things to do, either put up more money or stop extending business.

Conservatism takes alarm and issues imperative orders to reduce lines, and to stop expansion. It is possible that the present is not a good time to extend business in the United States. As to that there may be two opinions, but there cannot be any doubt that if the years from 1879 to 1882 inclusive were good ones in which to expand, the present is better, because rates are better. If it will pay to sell insurance on a falling market it will certainly pay to sell it when the market is going up.

More than this, to continue to sell is the only hope that these companies can have to get out whole. They have loaded up with liabilities at a low rate of premium, which they must meet. Some of them have put into that "terrible factor the unexpired risk" a large portion of their capital, and it does not seem to us the part of wisdom to sit down and let it devour their substance.

Let us see how much of a shower it is which has caused our British friends to put up their umbrellas and start for shelter. We shall leave out the older companies—that is older in American business—though some of them are worse scared than the new ones. There are, as we have said, nine British companies that have established branches here since 1879. They have been here an average of three years. They have sent to this country *net*, the sum of 5,136,000 dols. Their surplus above all liabilities is 3,506,000 dols.

They appear, therefore, to have planted in agencies and supplies and in establishing a business, the sum of 1,630,000 dols. besides the loss of interest. The salvage on unpaid and unsettled losses, which are reported as gross will go far to recover this latter loss.

What have they got for their million and a half and over? First, the five millions they brought here and invested have grown to eight and a half millions at interest. Second, they have an annual premium income of over six and a half millions. To have achieved this position in three years with rates what they have been during the time, at an expense of a million and a half of dollars, seems to us to call for rejoicing and not for despondency.

We have no expectation that the British managers will change their tactics at our suggestion. At the same time we cannot but see that they have not exhibited the pluck we expected of them, and that they have put their American managers in a very unpleasant position. The latter have incurred large expenses in building up a business which they are now compelled to relinquish just as they are getting into a position to obtain something from it. They are obliged to see business go off their books on which they have made nothing when they could put it back at a profit. And in the end they will have to take the blame of the losses which they cannot avert. Fire insurance in the United States will well repay a more careful study by the British managers.—*Weekly Underwriter*, New York.

Nous avons été favoré avec le premier nombre d'un journal intitulé, " l'Agent d'Assurances," édité par M. C. Marrhem. Pour la France l'idée est originale, et si le nombre que nous avons réçu peut être pris pour un specimen, on peut considéré le papier un succés.

Laughing.—God made us to laugh as well as to cry. The laugh of a little child will make the holiest day more sacred still. Strike with hand of fire, O weird musician, thy harp strung with Apollo's hair! Fill the vast cathedral aisles with symphonies sweet and dim, deft teacher of the organ keys! Blow, bugler, blow, until thy silver notes do touch and kiss the moonlit waves, charming the wandering lovers on the vine-clad hills, but know your sweetest strains are discords all compared with childhood's happy laugh—the laugh that fills the eye with light, and dimples every cheek with joy. Oh, rippling river of laughter, thou art the blessed boundary line between the beast and the man, and every wave of time doth draw a more fretful field of care.

QUEEN
INSURANCE COMPANY,

CHIEF OFFICES:—

QUEEN INSURANCE BUILDINGS, LIVERPOOL; and 60, GRACECHURCH ST., LONDON.

Twenty-sixth Annual Report and Fifth Quinquennium.

The Report and Accounts for the year 1883, presented to the Shareholders at the ANNUAL MEETING, on TUESDAY, 20TH MAY, 1884, shewed in the

FIRE BRANCH,

That the premiums for 1883 after deducting Reinsurances, amounted to £589,310 and the losses to £409,614.

In the LIFE BRANCH,

That new Policies had been issued for £270,973, yielding in premiums £9,064, and that the Life Fund was increased by £50,291, being the largest addition made in any year since the Company was established.

That the Quinquennial Valuation just completed, had been made on the strictest principles and was of the most searching character, nothing in the shape of future profit being anticipated.

That the Reversionary Bonus to participants amounted to One pound ten shillings per cent. per annum on the sum assured, or Seven pounds ten shillings per cent. on policies in force for five full years on 31st December last.

The surplus in the year's accounts, amounting to £50,861 2s. 8d., was disposed of as follows:—

£8,700	ADDED TO FIRE FUND.
18,003	APPROPRIATED FOR DIVIDEND.
24,157	CARRIED FORWARD TO NEXT ACCOUNT.

The FUNDS

Were shewn thereafter to stand as follows:—

Capital Paid-up	£180,035
Reserves	334,455
Life Accumulation Fund	455,579
Annuity Fund	14,549
TOTAL FUNDS IN HAND	**£1,087,763**

THE AUDITORS' REPORT, DATED 14th MAY, 1884, STATED:—

"We have examined the Books of the Queen Insurance Company, with the Vouchers and Securities, including the Certificates sent home from the American and Australian Branches for their investments. We have also examined the Audited Balance Sheets of the Foreign Branches, and we certify that the combined Balance Sheet exhibits a full and accurate view of the Company's position on the 31st December, 1883, as shewn by the Books.

"The present aggregate market value of the Securities is largely in excess of the cost appearing in the Balance Sheet."

HARMOOD, BANNER & SON, *Chartered Accountants.*

The Income of the Company is now	£710,851
The Company has paid in satisfaction of Claims	£4,889,220

J. MONCRIEFF WILSON, *General Manager.*
T. WALTON THOMSON, *Sub-Manager.*
J. K. RUMFORD, *Secretary in London.*

ACTIVE AND INFLUENTIAL AGENTS WANTED.

London and Lancashire Fire Insurance Company,

ESTABLISHED 1862.

CAPITAL FULLY SUBSCRIBED, £1,852,000.

HEAD OFFICE: 11, Dale Street, LIVERPOOL; LONDON OFFICE: 74, King William Street, E.C.

With Numerous Branches and Agencies throughout the World.

RESULTS OF 1883.

Copies of the Report for the Year 1883 may be obtained from any of the Company's Offices or Agencies

The Fire Premiums for 1883, after deducting re-insurances, amounted to	£490,000 7 10
The Fire Losses for the year, after making ample provisions for all losses occurring up to 31st December, were	324,978 14 3
After deducting all Commissions and Expenses, including Interest on Investments and other Receipts, the business of the year shows a balance to the Company's credit on the year's transactions of £43,289 3s. 8d. To this has to be added £35,682 0s. 10d., balance from 1882, making a total of	78,971 4 6
Out of which £20,000 has been carried to Reserve, increasing that fund to	230,000 0 0
After payment of Dividends (Free of Income Tax) of 8 per cent., absorbing £14,816, there has been carried forward to next year's Account the sum of	44,155 4 6

SECURITY.

Capital Paid up	185,200 0 0
Reserve Funds (excluding Capital)	274,155 4 6
Reserved Capital at call of Directors	1,666,800 0 0

CHAS. G. FOTHERGILL, Manager,
J. B. MOFFAT, Sub-Manager.

The Directors invite application for Agencies in Towns and Districts where the Company is not fully represented, and are also open to receive applications from those at present representing Life Companies only.

London : Printed by PAGE & PRATT, 5, 6 & 7, Ludgate Circus Buildings, E.C.—May 1, 1884.

PLATE GLASS INSURANCE COMPANIES.

SPECTATOR

THE INSURANCE — OF LONDON

MY TABLETS—MEET IT IS, I SET IT DOWN—*Hamlet.*

No. 80.—Vol. VII.   DECEMBER 1, 1884.   SEMI-MONTHLY 4d.

SCRAPS.

Exchanges will oblige by noting that our address is, and has been for some time—5, Ludgate Circus Buildings, London, E.C.

The chief officers of insurance companies are respectfully invited to send early notice of annual meetings, in order that our reporter may attend.

Why are dull times the best for advertising? Because, when money is scarce, people are forced to economise; they then read the advertisements to see who sells the cheapest, and where they can buy to the best advantage.

Almost a Tragedy; or, The Song of "Insurance Receipts."

Class, number, benefit, date, premium, name,
From morning to evening—'tis always the same,
Turning one over—beginning again,
Hech! writing receipts is a plague and a pain.
Class, number, benefit, till the hand won't move,
Date, premium, name, in the same old groove;
Class, till the eye gets weary and dim,
Premium, till cramped are the fingers and limb.
Who that has written from morning till night,
Has not felt disgusted and worried outright;
The tread-mill gives scope to the muscular man,
The eel may leap in the frying pan,
But the insurance clerk! ah, me, for his fate,
He must jog ever on, with class, benefit, date!

Now and again a deep-drawn sigh,
Once in a while a large tear in his eye,
Tell of the grinding receipts on "his brain,"
Speak of his labour, his worry, and pain.
                              "AMICUS CERTUS."
St. Vincent Place, Glasgow.

In the Faubourg Saint Honore:—
"Listen, baby, the good God has brought you a little brother." "Oh! I'm so glad. Does mamma know it?"

A story is told of a man who insured 1,000 cigars valued at £40 against fire and water. After the lapse of six months he made his appearance at the insurance office and demanded his money, as the cigars had been burned. "But not on board the vessel, sir?" said the secretary, "for she is in the dock now."—"Yes, on board the vessel. I smoked them, and therefore burned them all, myself, and the insurance says against fire." The secretary was taken aback, but told the smoker to come back again the next day. He called at the appointed time, but was met by the solicitor of the company, who told him that if he did not relinquish his claim, he would be prosecuted as one who had knowingly and wilfully set fire to goods insured by the company.

A traveller, seeing three strong, lazy fellows lounging under a hedge said, "Come, now, which will earn a shilling for being the laziest?" "I am the laziest, sir," said the first man, getting up and touching his hat. "I'm lazier than him, sir," said the second, making no effort to rise. "Here, my man," said the gentleman to the third, who had neither moved nor spoken; "the shilling

Personals.

Mr. A. Williamson has resigned the London managership of the *Northern* Accident Insurance Company, Limited.

Mr. Joseph Spencer, late of the *National Provident*, has been appointed inspector of agents for the *Economic*, London district.

Mr. A. Musgrave has been appointed to represent the *British Empire Mutual*, in the Leeds district.

Mr. John Runtz, chairman of the *British Empire* Life Assurance Company, who has just returned from Canada, has, in his absence, been elected a director of the New River Company.

Mr. Charles J. Brightling, of the *Royal* Insurance Company, has been appointed chief clerk for the London office of the *Kent* Insurance Company.

Mr. Bruce Morison, of 4, Broad Street-buildings, London, E.C., has been appointed manager of the company, *Les Assurances Belges* of Brussels.

Multum in Parvo.

☞ **THE GUARANTEE SOCIETY**, during the rebuilding of their premises at 19, Birchin-lane, are carrying on business at temporary offices, 38, Nicholas-lane, Lombard-street, E.C.

☞ **UNION INDUSTRIAL ACCIDENT AND GENERAL ASSURANCE COMPANY, LIMITED.**—This Company was registered on the 1st, with a capital of £25,000 in £1 shares, to transact Employers' Liability, Accident, Guarantee, Cattle, Plate Glass, and other insurance business. The founder is Mr. Walter Brainbridge, of 2½, Plevna-road, Stamford-hill, who, in the event of the Company going to allotment, is to receive £1,000 in cash, in consideration of the payment of preliminary expenses and for other services.

☞ **NEW COMPANY.—GENERAL TRAVELLERS' ASSURANCE.**—Objects: To carry on the business of an accident insurance company in all its branches. Capital: £2,000, in £20 shares. Signatories (with one share each): A. D. Keates, 15, Raymouth-road; W. Weller, 34, Ellesmere-road; G. Hunstour, 200, Cambridge-road, Kilburn; C. W. P. Overend, 6, South-square, Gray's Inn; C. Clark, 160, Cambridge-road, Kilburn; J. Barker, 19, Sistora-road, Balham; R. C. Heddell, 18, Telegraph-street. The number of directors to be not less than three nor more than ten. Remuneration, £200 per annum, each. Registered by F. Simpson, 45, Percy-road, Kilburn.

☞ **BRITISH EMPIRE MUTUAL LIFE.**—Three gentlemen from the home office of this Company have recently visited Canada, namely, Messrs. John Runtz, chairman, who is also a prominent member of the London Metropolitan Board of Works; Edwin Bowley, secretary, who was formerly connected with the Liverpool and London and Globe Office; and Samuel Walker, the surveyor generally employed by the Company; this gentleman ranks high in his profession in London, and his name is well known in connection with the building of the Law Courts in that city. They highly approved of the purchase of the Exchange Bank premises, as well as of the other investments made by Mr. Stancliffe in Canada for his Company. They seemed greatly pleased with their visit to Canada, and expressed much satisfaction with the business and future prospects of the British Empire in the Dominion.—*Insurance Society*, Montreal.

☞ **INSURANCE AND ACTUARIAL SOCIETY OF GLASGOW.**—Mr. J. Wyllie Guild, C.A., President of the Society, has offered a prize of £10 for the best essay on "The future finance of life and fire insurance with reference to rates of interest and expenses." The following are the conditions of the competition:—1. That the competition shall be open to all who are members of the Society on 1st December, 1884, with the exception of managers and secretaries of insurance companies, actuaries, and chartered accountants. 2. That the essays, which must not be in the handwriting of the competitor, shall be sent to the secretary of the Society on or before the second day of February, 1885. 3. That the essays sent in shall become the property of the Society, subject to the following provision of bye-law No. 8, viz. :—" Any papers not published by the Society within six months may then be published by the author." 4. That along with each essay there shall be sent to the secretary a sealed envelope containing the name of the competitor, and having on the outside a motto corresponding to one to be affixed to the head of the essay. Such motto not to be in the handwriting of the competitor. 5. That the prize shall not be awarded unless the committee shall consider some essay worthy of the distinction.

"JOHN BULL" AND "EMPIRE" INSURANCE COMPANIES.

WE notice by the London *Insurance Spectator* that the *John Bull* Insurance Company, Limited, of that city, is advertising to furnish "fire insurance at home and abroad at current rates." It is organised on a capital of £2,000 in 2,000 shares of £1 each, and on the 3rd of March last had ten shares taken and ten pounds sterling paid up. The *Spectator* has been informed by the manager that "more money has been paid in since that date," but how little more the manager failed to disclose. As the Company is ready to operate "abroad" a fine opening is offered to some enterprising gentleman to establish an agency for it at Washington, D.C. Where the *City* and *Provincial* and the *Anglo-American* make their lair the *John Bull* should find congenial company. Thus the phrases, "thick as thieves" and "thick as three in a bed," would be enriched with new and happy significance.—*Insurance*, New York.

Quite recently an "*Empire* Fire Insurance Company" was announced—under the most unpromising conditions—and in the course of a conversation the other day with a broker, I was shown a policy written to cover an American risk, and purporting to be issued by the "*Empire* Accident Company (Fire Department)"—quite a novel combination, by the way—and evidently written by the gentleman who subscribed as manager. The policy was numbered 1,001 (in other words 1) and a demand for return premium and cancellation was refused. Naturally! The company was evidently one formed for the purpose of doing business as far as collection of premiums and payment of manager's salary, &c., was concerned—such questions as return premiums and payment of losses would have to be met at a future period; but I scarcely imagine that payment of these last is *certain!*—Extract from letter of London to *Insurance Monitor*, New York.

ROYAL LIVER FRIENDLY SOCIETY.

GENERAL ACCOUNT, 31ST DECEMBER, 1883.
BURIAL BRANCH.—*Dr.*

	£ s. d.	£ s. d.	£ s. d.
To Paid Claims and Grants		.. ..£175,897 9 8	
„ Amount set aside under Rule 47, being 40 per cent. out of £280,402 1s. 0½d., being the contributions of old members ..	£112,160 16 5		
„ Amount set aside under amendment to Rule 47, being 80 per cent. out of £55,364 3s., being the contributions of new members..	44,291 6 5		
„ Amount set aside under Rule 47, being 30 per cent. out of £3,887 15s. 2½d., being the contributions under Tables 4, 5, 6, and 7, Schedule B	1,166 6 7		
„ Amount set aside under Rule 47, being entrance fees paid by members	3,292 8 4½		
		160,910 17 9½	
„ Balance		35,513 16 8½	
		£372,322 4 2	

BURIAL BRANCH.—*Cr.*

	£ s. d.	£ s. d.
By Collections for twelve months..	£343,152 10 0½	
„ Less returned to rejected members	206 2 5	
		£342,946 7 7½

INTEREST ACCOUNT.

	less Income Tax	£ s. d.	£ s. d.	£ s. d.
, Mersey Docks and Harbour Board			1,682 9 9	
„ Swansea Harbour Trust .. .. .. „ „ ..			1,586 4 11	
', Govan Hill Commissioners .. .. .. „ „			166 10 0	
', Birkenhead Commissioners .. .. .. „ „			306 9 5	
„ South Staffordshire Mines Drainage Commissioners „ „			790 18 5	
„ Corporation of Bradford (Yorkshire) .. „ „			414 16 4	
„ „ „ (Lancashire) .. „ „			112 7 8	
„ „ Batley .. „ „			826 19 8	
„ „ Bristol (Docks) .. „ „			194 11 8	
„ „ Cardiff .. „ „			1,070 6 9½	
„ „ Southampton .. „ „			175 11 9	
„ „ Sheffield .. „ „			389 3 4	
„ „ Southport .. „ „			496 3 9	
„ „ Wigan .. „ „			826 19 6	
„ Birkenhead Board of Guardians .. „ „			96 1 6	
„ Everton Burial Board .. „ „			1,371 3 2	
„ West Derby Local Board .. „ „			1,819 19 8½	
„ Great Crosby „ „ „			763 16 4	
„ Dalton-in-Furness „ .. „ „			283 17 4	
„ Chadderton „ .. „ „			105 15 6	
„ Wallasey „ .. „ „			1,762 10 0	
„ East Barnett Valley Local Board .. „ „			41 7 0	
„ Whitehaven Board of Guardians .. „ „			566 12 0	
„ Wirral „ „ .. „ „			49 2 10½	
„ Oldham „ „ .. „ „			304 5 10	
„ Bridlington Local Board .. „ „			440 12 4	
„ Osset-cum-Gawthorpe Local Board .. „ „			240 5 8	
„ Smethwick „ „ .. „ „			2,244 1 5½	
„ London and North Western Railway Company „ „			10 18 9	
„ Tyne Improvement Commissioners .. .. „ „			1,240 9 4	
„ Herne Bay Commissioners .. .. „ „			213 10 2½	
„ Tees Conservancy .. .. .. „ „			1,244 9 0	
„ Medway Conservancy .. .. „ „			2,894 8 7	
„ Barton, Eccles, Winton, and Monton Burial Board „ „			434 5 3	
„ Brimington Burial Board .. .. „ „			182 8 5	
„ Liverpool Select Vestry .. .. „ „			110 17 10	
„ Atherstone School Board .. .. „ „			150 2 6	
„ Hull, Barnsley, and West Riding Junction Railway and Dock Company.. .. .. „ „			787 3 9	
„ King's Lynn Dock Company .. .. „ „			493 2 0	
„ Income Tax recovered	£2 13 11			
„ Income Tax outstanding	719 13 7			
			722 7 6	
„ Proportion of interest outstanding (on investments) to date, for portions of periods unexpired	2,841 16 10			
Deduct amount outstanding interest 31st Dec., 1882	2,347 16 3			
			494 0 7	
„ Mortgages—Interest	1,481 16 1			
Rents from forfeited properties	519 12 3			
			2,001 8 4	
„ Savings Banks—Liverpool	563 19 7			
„ „ Glasgow	312 2 6			
„ „ Dublin	4 7 0			
			880 9 1	
			30,989 4 9½	
Deduct amount transferred to endowment fund			2,531 3 0	
				28,458 1 9½
„ Amount charged management fund for rent of premises in Prescot-street .. .:				917 14 9
				£372,322 4 2

MANAGEMENT FUND ACCOUNT, 31ST DECEMBER, 1883.

To commission on contributions (including extra commission on all new business entered from 30th June, 1875), burial branch	..£88,138 17 1½		
„ Entrance fees to collectors, burial branch ..	3,291 9 11		
„ Amounts to agents, collectors, and canvassers on new business, burial branch	13,532 15 7½		
„ Agents and collectors for transferring names to new books	2,032 18 3½		
		£106,996 0 11½	
„ Board of management and treasurer		10,212 0 0	
„ Clerks, agents, &c.		24,591 6 0½	
„ Travelling expenses of agents and committee		1,712 3 4	
„ Printing, stationery, advertising, &c.	5,530 18 7		
Less received for rule books, &c.	231 14 11		
		5,299 3 8	
„ Postage stamps, money orders, bank commission, carriage of parcels, &c. ..		3,234 12 8½	
„ Agents' rents, taxes, insurance, &c.		1,887 2 3	
„ Amount credited income for rent of premises in Prescot-street (at average rate of interest on investments), on cost to date		917 14 9	
„ Repairs		177 18 10	
„ Solicitor's salary, and other law charges		1,358 16 11	
„ Actuary for services		105 0 0	
„ Accountants for services		650 0 0	
„ Doctors for examinations		2,036 15 5	
„ Trustees' remuneration		315 0 0	
„ Subscriptions to charities		73 10 0	
„ Balance		22,252 5 8	
		£181,819 10 6½	

By Balance per last account			£20,896 10 5
„ Amount set aside under Rule 47, being 40 per cent. on the contributions of old members, £280,402 1s. 0½d.	£112,160 16 5		
„ Amount set aside under amendment of Rule 47, being 80 per cent. on the contributions of new members, £55,364 3s.	44,291 6 5		
„ Amount set aside under Rule 47, being 30 per cent. out of £3,887 15s. 2½d., being the contributions under Tables 4, 5, 6, and 7, Schedule B	1,166 6 7		
„ Amount set aside under Rule 47, being entrance fees paid by members ..	3,292 8 4½		
		160,910 17 9½	
„ Medical aid—Collections for twelve months		536 9 8½	
Less commission	£86 19 5½		
„ Doctors' salaries	437 7 11		
		524 7 4½	
		12 2 4	
		£181,819 10 6½	

BALANCE SHEET, 31ST DECEMBER, 1883.

To Cash in Savings Bank, Liverpool	..£38,914 7 4	
„ „ „ Glasgow	.. 11,663 19 3	
„ „ „ Dublin	.. 179 1 5	
		£50,757 8 0

BONDS, &c.

„ Mersey Docks and Harbour Board	.. 38,429 3 4	
„ Swansea Harbour Trust	.. 36,000 0 0	
„ Trustees Maryport Improvement (Harbour) Act..	.. 10,000 0 0	
„ King's Lynn Dock Company	.. 25,000 0 0	
„ Medway Conservancy..	.. 69,786 17 9	
„ Govan Hill Commissioners	.. 3,579 17 0	
„ Birkenhead „	.. 7,000 0 0	
„ Tyne Improvement „	.. 30,000 0 0	
„ Herne Bay „	.. 5,000 0 0	
„ Tees Conservancy „	.. 30,000 0 0	
„ South Staffordshire Mines Drainage Commissioners	.. 18,000 0 0	
„ Liverpool Select Vestry	.. 2,244 19 9	
„ Everton Burial Board..	.. 31,879 6 7	
„ Barton, Eccles, Winton, and Monton Burial Board	.. 10,060 0 0	
„ Brimington Burial Board	.. 4,050 0 0	
„ Birkenhead Board of Guardians	.. 1,948 1 6	
„ Whitehaven „	.. 12,807 13 2	
„ Wirral „	.. 1,111 15 7½	
„ Oldham „	.. 6,600 0 0	
„ London and North Western Railway Co.	.. 150 0 0	
„ Hull, Barnsley, and West Riding Junction Railway and Dock Co. ..	.. 20,000 0 0	
„ Corporation of Batley..	.. 20,000 0 0	
„ „ Bradford (Lancashire)	.. 2,345 10 0	
„ „ „ (Yorkshire)	.. 10,000 0 0	
„ „ Bristol..	.. 5,000 0 0	
„ „ Cardiff	.. 24,245 3 0	
„ „ Sheffield	.. 10,000 0 0	
„ „ Southport	.. 12,000 0 0	
„ „ Southampton	.. 4,099 13 5	
„ „ Wigan..	.. 20,000 0 0	
„ Smethwick Local Board	.. 55,368 13 8	

„ Dalton-in-Furness Local Board	..	..	..	..	..	..	5,865 14 8	
„ Great Crosby „	..	..	..	..	..	..	16,949 4 7	
„ Bridlington „	..	..	..	..	..	..	10,858 10 2	
„ Wallasey „	..	..	..	..	..	..	40,000 0 0	
„ West Derby „	..	..	..	..	..	..	40,383 4 5	
„ Chadderton „	..	..	..	..	..	..	2,500 0 0	
„ Osset-cum-Gawthorpe „	..	..	..	..	..	..	5,620 12 9	
„ Atherstone School Board	..	..	..	..	..	..	3,592 1 10	
								652,476 3 2½
„ Mortgages per last account	..	..	..	..	..	..	33,115 0 0	
Less paid off	..	..	..	£1,800 0 0				
„ transferred to forfeited property ..	..	..	..	800 0 0				
							2,600 0 0	
								30,515 0 0
„ Forfeited property per last account	..	..	..	..	..	19,758 6 8		
Add amount transferred from mortgages	..	..	..	..	..	800 0 0		
							20,558 6 8	
„ Office fixtures and furniture in head office as now valued ..	..	..	..	3,657 16 4				
„ „ „ branch offices „	..	..	..	1,594 4 7½				
							5,252 0 11½	
„ Freehold property in Prescot-street	..	..	..	..	..	..	28,223 16 2	
„ Balance debit of agents ..	..	..	..	..	..	6,440 15 11½		
Less at credit of agents	..	..	..	..	..	13 12 3		
							6,427 3 8½	
„ Interest outstanding on new investments to 31st December	..	..	..	2,841 16 10				
„ Income tax outstanding ..	..	..	..	..	..	719 13 7		
„ Cash in treasurer's hands	..	..	..	..	..	772 11 2		
								£798,544 0 3½
By amount at credit of burial branch, 31st December	..	..	..	.. £675,794 5 10				
„ Balance of general account to date	..	..	..	..	..	35,513 16 8½		
								£711,308 2 6½
„ Amount at credit of endowment fund, 31st December	..	..	..	61,096 14 4				
Add interest at average rate of investments	..	..	..	2,531 3 0				
							63,627 17 4	
„ Collections for twelve months ..	..	..	..	..	£11,939 7 4			
Less claims paid ..	..	..	.. £11,285 15 3½					
„ Commission ..	..	..	.. 1,477 9 2½					
					12,763 4 6			
							823 17 2	
							62,804 0 2	
„ Management fund ..	..	..	..	..	..	..	22,252 5 8	
„ Outstanding accounts ..	..	..	..	..	..	..	2,179 11 11	
								£798,544 0 3½

We have audited the accounts, and satisfied ourselves of the existence of the securities. The valuations upon which the mortgages were taken by the committee of management were those of Mr. William Culshaw, Messrs. Picton, Chambers, and Bradley, and Messrs. Audsley, surveyors, Liverpool, and revalued by Mr. Henry Sumners.

(Signed)   WELCH AND PARKINSON, *Chartered Accountants.*

Liverpool, *5th May,* 1884.

Argus Eye-tems.

FLIES should make good actuaries, judging from the way they multiply.

WHY is a Zulu belle like a prophet? Because she has not much on'er in her own country. Where was the insurance agent?

WHEN we read in an exchange—" Mt. Sterling, Ill., having voted in favour of local option and completed a jail, is prepared to take care of all inebriates. The young insurance agent, Mr. ———, is making a fair start in business," are we to suppose that young Mr. ———is a hard drinker?

CAPTAIN SHAW thinks our fire engines and appliances have so many improvements (?) put on them that they are unwieldly and not so good as they would otherwise be.

THE difference as given between the House of Commons and the House of Lords, might be applied to the difference between the management of some insurance companies—all the difference between ability and no'bility.

ABOUT this time, it is said that the proprietor of a summer hotel calls to his porter—" Sam, have the kerosene oil all fixed, and the dynamite in place!" "Yes, sir, all ready." "How about the policies of insurance; are they all in the safe and it securely locked?" "Yes, sir." "Well, let her off, we might as well close the season right away."

MRS. JOBBLESWIZZLE was looking over some insurance statistics, and noticing the difference between the summer and winter reports, she said to her husband: "Jobbleswizzle, I see by these figures that there are much greater losses by fire in winter than in summer. Can you tell me why?" "I presume, my love, it is because there are more fires in winter than in summer." "Of course, smarty," she answered in a vexed tone, "I am aware of that, but why are there more?" "Because, love, you know it is too warm in the summer to have fires. Have you kept house all this time and didn't know that." Mrs. J. did not appear to be satisfied with the explanation, and she steadily scratched her dome of thought.

THE NATIONAL MUTUAL LIFE ASSOCIATION OF AUSTRALASIA, LIMITED.

REPORT OF THE DIRECTORS

On the Fourth Investigation of the Affairs of the Association, presented to the Members at an Extraordinary General Meeting, held at the Melbourne Athenæum, Collins-street, Melbourne, on Wednesday, 16th July, 1884.

Your directors have now the pleasure to submit to the members the report of the actuary on the fourth investigation of the affairs of the Association, embracing the three years ending 30th September, 1883.

The investigation has been completed by Mr. J. M. Templeton, who, although he resigned his position as manager of the Association in February last, agreed to carry on and complete the trienniel investigation on which he was then engaged.

The method of valuation and the mode of dividing profits are the same as those adopted at previous investigations.

The valuation balance - sheet shows a surplus of £40,109 11s. 11d. in the assurance fund, £1,352 6s. 3d. in the endowment fund, and £22 7s. 10d. in the annuity fund.

As no part of the guarantee fund created at last investigation has been required, the share of every member therein will now be apportioned. In cases where death has occurred during the past triennium, the representatives of the deceased will receive the amount in cash ; and in cases where the policies are still in force, it will be converted into a reversionary bonus, and added to the policy. Of the surplus of £40,109 11s. 11d. in the assurance branch, the directors have set apart £5,000 as a guarantee fund for the next three years, the share of every member therein being ascertained and reserved until next investigation ; and £35,000 has been ordered to be divided among the members whose polices are dated previous to 1st October, 1882 ; the balance, £109 11s.11d., being carried forward to next triennium.

In the endowment branch, £1,000 has been ordered to be divided among the members of that branch whose policies are dated before the 1st October, 1882, and £352 6s. 3d. has been caried forward to next triennium.

The surplus in the annuity branch of £22 7s. 10d. has been ordered to be carried forward to next triennium.

The directors congratulate the members on the very satisfactory results shown by this fourth investigation, and on the substantial amount of bonus added to the policies.

EDWARD LANGTON, Chairman.

Melbourne, 12th July, 1884.

REPORT BY THE ACTUARY

On the investigation of the affairs of the Association, as at 30th September, 1883.

I.—INTRODUCTORY NARRATIVE.

In presenting to the members this my fourth investigation report on the affairs of the Association, I follow my usual custom of giving as an introduction a short narrative of the progress of the Association during the period elapsed since the date of my last report—viz., from 1st October, 1880, to 30th September, 1883.

The success which followed the establishment of branch offices in New South Wales, South Australia, and New Zealand, encouraged your directors vigorously to prosecute the work of extension. Acting under their instructions, immediately after I had completed the third division of profits I proceeded to Tasmania, to make office arrangements for a branch in that colony. The chairman of your directors (Mr. Langton) had previously secured leading men of business in Hobart to act as local directors. I inaugurated the establishment of the office in that city by delivering a lecture in the Town Hall, on "The Theory of Life Assurance." The Mayor of Hobart presided, and His Excellency the Governor and the members of the Government of Tasmania did me the honour of being present. I had an audience of twelve hundred people, who seemed to be much interested with the diagrams which I exhibited and the explanations which I gave. A full report, occupying three or four columns, appeared in the next morning's paper ; and I left the branch office in Hobart in full working order under an influential local board and a resident secretary, with every prospect of success, which has since been fully realised.

Soon afterwards I proceeded to Queensland. In that colony the Association was almost unknown, but after three months' work I think the people knew a little about the Association and the liberality of its principles. I spent most of the time in Brisbane, but I also visited Toowomba, Maryborough, Rockhampton, and Townsville, where I succeeded in gaining the interest of some of the leading people. I secured four of the leading men of that colony as local directors, engaged the services of a resident secretary of great energy and experience, and rented commodious offices in Queen-street (the principal street in Brisbane), and business was commenced in real earnest. I wound up by delivering the same lecture in Brisbane as I did in Hobart. Sir Arthur Palmer, K.C.M.G., presided, and, although the night was wet, I had an audience of more than six hundred, who received me well, and listened to me attentively. All the newspapers contained full reports of my lecture, thus forming an appropriate termination to my efforts in disseminating information respecting the Association. The business transacted at this branch office has far exceeded my anticipations.

As the local directors in South Australia (acting under the authority of your directors) had previously established a branch office in Fremantle, Western Australia, the Association entered on its thirteenth year with an organisation co-extensive with its name, and became, in fact, The National Mutual Life Association of Australasia, forming a complete business federation of the Australasian Colonies. The thirteenth year was also distinguished as the first in which the new business exceeded one million pounds sterling in amounts assured, the excess in that and the fourteenth year making the average annual amount of new business during the triennium more than one million, a result upon which I congratulate the members as an unparalleled success.

During the triennium the Association has acquired freehold property for the offices of the Association in Melbourne, Adelaide, Wellington (New Zealand), and Brisbane, in most central positions. The site in Brisbane is about fifty feet from the General Post Office, and on it is erected a substantial and ornamental building, with every convenience for the local board of directors and the office staff, and suites of offices, which are let to good tenants. In Adelaide the Association invited competitive designs for new offices, and the architect who received the first prize was commissioned to proceed with the work. The building has just been finished, and is pronounced to be one of the most beautiful in Adelaide, affording splendid accommodation for the business of the Association, and many suites of offices, which are expected to yield a handsome revenue from desirable tenants. It is situated in Victoria-square, about one hundred yards from the General Post Office. In Wellington a design has been adopted, and the contract let for the erection of a new building, which will be finished about the end of the present year, and will be an ornament to that city ; it is situated at the corner of two of the principal streets, and is about one hundred and fifty yards from the General Post Office.

The site of the head office is at the corner of Collins and Queen-streets, and is, in my opinion, the very best for the purpose in Melbourne. It was bought subject to a lease, which will expire in a few years, when your directors hope to be able to erect a building in every way worthy of the site and of the Association.

These freehold properties not only secure to you most desirable offices for all time, but they form permanent investments of the most valuable kind. Already their market value exceeds the amount expended on them by several thousands of pounds, for which no credit is taken in the accounts.

Since the date of my last report, the articles of association under which your business is conducted have been subjected to careful revision. I gave very long and patient consideration to the matter, and your directors had the subject under discussion very frequently. Many amendments which experience suggested, and alterations which the great extension of the business necessitated, were introduced. These alterations and amendments were adopted, and confirmed by you at extraordinary general meetings called for the purpose, and have now the full force of law.

(1) INCREASE OF BUSINESS.

The following table exhibits the number and amount of proposals received, and the number and amount of proposals declined or not completed, during each of the years now under review, viz. :—

Year ending	Received.		Declined, or not completed.	
	No. of Proposals.	Amounts Proposed.	No. of Proposals.	Amounts Proposed.
		£		£
30th September, 1881	5,166	1.304,978	1,475	412,204
„ „ 1882	6,127	1,546,812	1,572	437,324
„ „ 1883	5,995	1,606,657	1,702	524,950
Total	17,288	£4,458,517	4,749	£1,374,478

The number of policies issued, the amount assured, and the annual premium income derivable therefrom, are exhibited in the following

SUMMARY OF NEW BUSINESS TRANSACTED.

Year ending	No. of Policies issued	Amount Assured.	Annual Premiums.	Single Premiums.
		£	£ s. d.	£ s. d.
30th Sept., 1881	3,691	892,774	30,171 8 1	932 0 4
„ 1882	4,555	1,109,558	36,651 14 11	500 0 0
„ 1883	4,293	1,081,707	36,145 5 5	425 6 8
Total ..	12,539	£3,084,039	£102,968 8 5	£1,857 7 0

Comparing these tables with those under the same headings published in the previous investigation reports, we find that in the three years now under review 17,288 proposals for £4,458,517 were received, as against 8,539 proposals for £2,120,054 during the previous three years, 3,411 proposals for £891,942 during the three years forming the second investigation period, and 1,796 proposals for £613,780 received during the first five years of business; while the new policies issued during each of the four periods, commencing with the first five years, numbered 1,141, 2,513, 5,780, and 12,539 respectively, thus indicating a most remarkable rate of progress. The new business of the triennium exceeded the business transacted by the Association during the whole of the eleven years of its previous history. The following is a summary for the four investigation periods :—

Period.	No. of Policies issued	Amount Assured.	Annual Premiums.	Single Premiums.
		£	£ s. d.	£ s. d.
1st period, 5 yrs	1,141	379,500	12,945 2 0	57 9 0
2nd „ 3 „	2,513	634,092	23,618 15 10	138 18 7
3rd „ 3 „	5,780	1,321,562	43,966 5 3	350 0 0
4th „ 3 „	12,539	3,084,039	102,968 8 5	1,857 7 0
Total, 14 yrs	21,973	£5,419,193	£183,498 11 6	£2,403 14 7

(2) EXTENSION OF AGENCIES.

As stated above, branch offices have been established during the triennium in Hobart, Brisbane, and Fremantle. With those previously reported as opened in Sydney, Adelaide, and Wellington, the Association now has (including the head office in Melbourne) seven principal offices for the transaction of its business, under the management of permanent officers, controlled by directors clothed with ample powers.

(To be continued.)

THE ACTUARY, No. 45.

MR. JAMES DODSON, F.R.S.

(Continued from page 103.)

SOME copies have another title-page, also of 1747, in which Wilcox alone is mentioned in the imprint. " This means (says De Morgan) that Wilcox took the risk off Dodson's hands within the year ; and thenceforward we no more find him publishing on his own account." The same writer says further of this work :

" With the exception of heavy calculators, to whom the ' Canon ' is occasionally useful — Benjamin Gompertz, for instance, who told me 40 years ago he was always wanting it—this table is worth three of the ' Canon ' to anybody. Whoever can catch a copy should keep it. The table of binomial co-efficients up to the 34th power is very useful. So is the table of specific gravities. The medley of coins, measures, regular solids, and polygons, roots, logarithms, common, hyperbolic, logistic, trigonometrical, etc., interest, annuities, etc., etc., though not extensive, are great friends at a pinch. For a single book to travel with, and a good chance for anything that can be wanted, I know only Mr. Willich's table which can compare with it. But Dodson's two or three words to each head in the preliminary index enable the user to find his table in a moment."

In 1747-8.—Vol I. of the " Repository," which was dedicated to De Moivre. " It is not a new custom for authors to dedicate their mathematical works to gentlemen who are the most illustrious ornaments of mathematical sciences ; and as the learned world have long since thought it justice to rank you among that number, it will," etc. There was nothing specially bearing upon our subject in that vol.

The 2nd vol. appeared in 1753, and therein were (inter alia) many curious questions relating to chances and lotteries ; and a great number of questions concerning annuities for lives and their reversions, etc. This vol. is considered to offer the fullest development of De Moivre's hypothesis extant.—Insurance Clycopædia.

(To be continued.)

You can't eat enough in a week to last you a year, and you can't advertise on that plan either.

TERMS OF SUBSCRIPTION.

ANNUAL Subscription (including postage), Paid in advance, 9s.

NOTICE TO CORRESPONDENTS.

All Communications intended for insertion to be addressed to the Editor, " The INSURANCE SPECTATOR OF LONDON," 5, Ludgate Circus Buildings, E.C.

THEATRES, &c.

Adelphi Theatre (Strand), "In the Ranks," 8; Empire (Leicester - square), "Dick," 7.45; Globe (Newcastle street), "The Private Secretary," 8; Lyceum (Strand), "Pygmalion and Galatea," 8; Prince's (Piccadilly), "Called Back," 9; Strand, "Our Boys," 8.30; Vaudeville (Strand), "Saints and Sinners," 8; Royal Aquarium, Promenade Concerts, 8; Maskelyne and Cooke (Egyptian Hall), 8; Health Exhibition, South Kensington, daily (Sundays excepted).

ANSWERS TO CORRESPONDENTS.

R. S.—1. Thoroughly respectable. 2. The *British Workman* Assurance Company is thoroughly sound.
Sigma.—We are making enquiries.

CONTENTS :

THE

Insurance Spectator of London.

OCTOBER 15, 1884.

THE CHIEF OFFICERS of insurance companies are respectfully invited to send early notice of annual meetings, in order that our reporter may attend.

THE statement that the *Vienna* Insurance Company has closed the London office is absolutely incorrect, and we regret that it found currency in our columns. The *Vienna* is an office of the highest repute, and the directors have not the slightest intention of retiring from England.

THE recent advance in Fire Premiums, and the reductions being made upon the amounts held, render the prospects of the *Patria Belgica*, and the *National* (of Toulouse) exceedingly good. Both these offices are established and doing well. The sole agents for the United Kingdom are Messrs. Baker and Breard, the former of whom is known as an insurance expert of the highest order. The *National* being a mutual company, the whole of the participating members are liable to make good any losses, but the English policies, being of the non-participating class, do not incur that liability. Beyond this protection, a special fund has been created by the issue of debentures equal to one-half of the premium income. In addition to the securities thus offered, it has been arranged that for the further protection of policy-holders in the United Kingdom, one-half of all premiums received by the London Agency will be deposited in a London bank, for the sole purpose of meeting claims in the United Kingdom. We do not usually recommend Continental offices, but these are reliable, sound, institutions.

OUR attention has recently been directed to the financial position and prospects of Industrial Insurance Companies and Friendly Societies. This branch of Life business is becoming more popular than ever. Large figures are not of themselves a test of real progress, and the payments being made by some of these companies appear to us to border upon the narrow line which separates safety from hazard and danger. We have before us at this moment the accounts of a company called the *Royal Liver*, having its head offices in Liverpool. During last year this Company received £343,000 in premiums, for obtaining which it paid in commission, &c., £141,000, and the accumulated fund appears to be only slightly in excess of two years' income. Now, while we admit that the cost of conducting this class of business is much greater than that required to carry on what is termed "ordinary" Life business, we submit to the directors of the *Royal Liver* the following important queries:—1st, Is no 40 per cent. too high a rate to pay for procuring and collecting a premium income under *any* circumstances? 2nd, Is it probable that the comparatively small proportion reserved for future and certain liabilities is sufficient to render the policyholders perfectly safe? There can be no difficulty in obtaining satisfaction upon these points, because the Consulting Actuary is more than capable of giving the information. To a great extent industrial insurance is on its trial, and it behoves the different offices to beware lest the growing rivalry destroy the element of safety only to be maintained in connection with prudent expenditure and sufficient reserves.

A DARK DEED.

IT was all Sophy's doing.

"Give yourself a bit of a rest in the country, John," she said; "the business will get along well enough under the head clerk till the hot weather's over. We will take a little house in the country. What we want—at least *you* do—is the fresh air of the open country. I declare you begin to look quite thin, John, dear. I'm really quite concerned about you."

I yielded with a good grace, and every evening for a week I came home to find Sophy with a dozen or so of advertisements of "Desirable Homes in the Country," marked for ready reference.

After a voluminous correspondence and several tours of inspection, we made a choice at last. It was a semi-detached villa in a secluded locality, and surrounded by commodious grounds thickly shaded with trees. The other house was occupied by a family who, the agent had said, had given the best of references, though he knew nothing of them personally.

The surrounding grounds were divided by a close fence which completely separated the portions pertaining to the respective halves of the villas; so, if we didn't care to cultivate our neighbours, we could easily keep aloof.

It was several days before we saw any of the adjoining occupants. The first of them encountered was a white-headed old man, whom I met one morning coming out as if for an early walk similar to that from which I was just returning. He was bent with years and very venerable in appearance, and the bow with which he returned my salute was full of courtesy.

At intervals glimpses were caught of the remaining inmates, who consisted of a dark, dyspeptic-looking man of thirty-five, or thereabouts, a cheery-faced little woman some five years younger, whom Sophy set down as the dark man's wife, and a dowdyish maid-of-all-work.

It was not long before we discovered one drawback to our new abode. The partition-wall was so thin that we could not help hearing all that passed on the other side. So it was ascertained that the dyspeptic man's name was Eldritch, the old gentleman's Mr. Harbine, and the servant-maid's Biddy; furthermore, that Mr. Harbine was Mrs. Eldritch's father, and that his life was insured for his daughter's benefit.

I had always had a special dislike of prying curiosity; and one evening, as Sophy sat knitting close to the communicative wall—her favourite position lately—with her eyes on her work and one ear cocked attentively, I was in the act of clearing my throat for a homily on the sin of over-inquisitiveness, when Sophy gave a start that nearly tumbled her from her chair. Her face turned white and her whole frame trembled.

"Good heavens! Come here quick, John, and listen to this!"

Sophy's terrified look drove the lecture from my head, and in an instant I was at her side with my ear as closely glued to the partition as her own.

"The poison has done its work effectually," said a voice which Sophy whispered was the dark man's.

"Thank goodness we're rid of the old nuisance at last!" returned another, which we agreed was the wife's.

"He's been a terrible pest, but he'll trouble us no more," replied the first.

Then the speakers must have moved away a little, or turned their backs, for the next words were lost—all, except something about "insurance money," in the man's voice.

What was to be done? I knew not if there was a magistrate in the neighbourhood, or where to find him if there was. Besides, Sophy, absolutely refused to be left alone while I went to search.

After much consultation we resolved upon a course of action. There was no danger of Eldritch or his wife trying to escape as long as they had no reason to believe themselves suspected. I had a friend in the detective force to whom I would telegraph from the village the first thing in the morning, to come immediately, as I had important business for him.

The next day was Sunday, and after sending my despatch, I resolved to keep as close a watch on our neighbours as was practicable without awakening their distrust.

It was verging towards ten o'clock, when through a chink in the division fence, at which I was keeping watch, concealed by the shrubbery, I saw the Eldritches, in Sunday garb, pass through their front gate, looking as placid as if that white-haired old man's murder were not upon their consciences.

I went out at our own gate and followed at a safe distance. The two walked along leisurely, the woman's hand on the man's arm, till they reached the village, and finally, a neat little church, which they entered.

I waited awhile, and then also went in. Judge of my surprise at seeing in the pulpit, in the act of giving out the opening hymn—whom do you think? As true as my name's John Hetley, it was none other than the dark-faced murderer! I could hardly repress a cry of indignation at such sacrilege; and when he went on to preach a sermon on the golden rule, full of brotherly kindness and benevolence, I sat in stupified amazement at the man's effrontery.

At the close of the service I resumed my watch till I had seen the reverend assassin and his wife enter their own door. Sophy and I listened at the wall, but no sounds were audible. The neighbouring inmates were either exercising extraordinary caution, or were in another part of the house.

My detective friend came on Monday morning. A few words revealed what I had to disclose.

"If they've murdered the old man for the insurance," said my friend, "it's singular that they should conceal his death, as they appear to be doing. They can't get the money without disclosing the man is dead, and every moment's delay would only tend to excite suspicion. It looks as if they had changed their minds about trying to get the insurance, and were now only intent on covering up their crime. I propose that we call at once on Eldritch, and that you confront him with your discovery before they've had time to hide the body."

Our ring was answered by the dowdyish servant, who, at our request, led us into Mr. Eldritch's presence. "A life has been taken in this house by poison!" I said, abruptly and impressively.

I expected to see the wretch quail with terror, but he didn't. He looked up calmly, but a little curiously, and with an amused smile, answered, "I admit the fact."

Was there ever such audacity?

"Where have you bestowed the body?" I demanded.

"Come and I'll show you," he replied, without a sign of trepidation.

Could the man be in his senses, or would he, after all, escape the gallows on a plea of insanity?

He rose and led the way to a back garden, we following. Then, removing a few spadefuls of earth, he revealed to our expectant eyes the swollen corpse—don't be startled—of a huge rat!

"The old scamp had pestered us a good while," said Mr. Eldritch, "and being too cunning to be trapped, and more than a match for the cat, at last I laid a dose of arsenic for him."

"Don't trifle with us!" I said; sternly. "I overheard you talking about insurance money at the same time I heard your confession of the poisoning. You'll hardly claim you had this creature's life insured?"

Mr. Eldritch's smile broadened.

"My wife and I have consulted several times of late," he replied, "about getting up the money to pay the forthcoming instalment on her father's policy, but you must have had pretty sharp ears to have heard us."

Before I had time to answer, the white-haired victim of the supposed murderer made his appearance on the scene, and greeted us with his accustomed bow.

As well as I could for my confusion, I hastened to make a clean breast of it to Mr. Eldritch, who laughed heartily and forgave my espionage in consideration of the motive. We got to be excellent friends afterwards, and I found him to be a very worthy gentleman.

----●----

"DEAL only with those who advertise—you will never lose by it."—*Benjamin Franklin.*

FIDELITY GUARANTEE INSURANCE.

(Continued from page 94.)

IN this same year was founded the first of the modern associations, especially established for carrying on the business of Fidelity Insurance, viz., The Guarantee Society of London. An early prospectus contained the following :—

"The Guarantee Society has been established to obviate the defects of the system of suretiship by private bondsmen, which is universally acknowledged to be attended with various inconveniences and objections; instances have constantly occurred in which persons of the highest respectability have been obliged to forego valuable appointments; from either the great difficulty of obtaining security, or a repugnance to place their relatives or friends and themselves under the obligations involved therein. The Guarantee Society undertakes, on the payment of a small premium per cent. per annum, to make good in case of default by fraud or dishonesty, any losses which may be sustained to an amount specifically named and agreed upon in their policy, and by such means obviates the necessity for private sureties as well as the obligations arising therefrom, which often prove as prejudicial to the best interest of employers as to the party seeking guarantee.

"Rate of premium 10s. per cent. per annum and upwards (according to the nature of the employment) on the amount of security required.

"No charge is made for stamp duty except in special cases: the usual legal expenses of surety bonus will therefore be entirely avoided by persons who enter on their respective duties under the guarantee of this Society."

The Society obtained the authority of a special Act of Parliament in 1842, under which date we shall notice its provisions.

The British Guarantee of Trust Company was projected during the same year, but did not mature.

Mr. Francis, in his "Annals, etc., of Life Assurance," 1853, says :—

"When this Company was first started in 1840 for insurance against loss by the dishonesty of clerks, there was a great objection raised. It was thought one of those vague and speculative undertakings of which England has seen so many, and one which would necessarily fail, because the master would hesitate to take an assistant who could only give the security of a commercial company. 'The moral security is wanting!' was the exclamation of all. It was vain to answer, that this objection pointed both ways, as the relative would often give the desired bond which a mercantile institution would refuse. Still the parrot reply was heard, and the solemn shake of the head was followed by 'The moral security—where is the moral security?' and was deemed sufficient to crush all argument derived from mere statistics. Time passed, and it was discovered that because a banker's clerk gave the security of a company he did not become a rogue, but he did

become independent. It was found too that the master could make his claim good on the company with far more promptitude that he could on a relative. It was nothing to say to a board of directors, 'I will have justice and my bond,' but it was something to say to a broken-hearted parent, 'Your son has ruined you as well as himself—discharge your obligation!' It is well-known that bankers and merchants have often foregone their due rather than thus reimburse their losses : and it has been found that notwithstanding the facts of the moral security being wanting, the societies which guarantee the master from loss by the servant have been very successful and very serviceable, and are on the increase."

1842.—There was passed this year what is technically designated a private Act of Parliament.—5 Vict. (Sess. 2) cap. lxiv.—" An Act for regulating legal proceedings by or against ' The Guarantee Society,' and for granting certain powers thereto." The majority of its provisions relate simply to the conduct of the business of that Association and will be noticed in its history ; but section xvi. enabled the Lords of the Treasury, and the head of Public Departments to accept the security of this Society, and so gave it a public character. The clause recites an Act passed in the 50 Geo. III. cap. 85, intituled—" An Act to regulate the taking of securities in all offices in respect of which security ought to be given, and for avoiding the grant of all such offices in the event of such security not being given within a time to be limited after the grant of such office," whereby it was enacted that every person who should after the passing of the Act be appointed to any office or employment, or commission, civil or military, in any public department in the United Kingdom or the Colonies, wherein he should be concerned in the collection, receipt, disbursement, or expenditure of any public moneys, was required to give security, as therein is provided ; and reciting the further Acts, 52 Geo. III. cap. 66 ; 6 & 7 Wm. IV. cap. 28 ; and 1 & 2 Vic. cap. 61, enlarging and amending the provisions of the first-named Act, it proceeds :

" And it is expedient, as well for the greater ease of persons required to give security as aforesaid, as for the better securing the public interest, that further provisions should be made in this respect : Be it therefore enacted, That from and after the passing of this Act it shall and may be lawful to and for the Lord High Treasurer and Commissioners of the Treasury, or any three or more of them, or the principal officer or officers of any other public office or department in which any person or persons shall be required to give security by bond or otherwise, as mentioned in the before-recited Acts, or either of them, to make and accept if he or they shall think fit, in lieu of such bond or other security, the guarantee or security of the said Guarantee Society, to be given and executed in and by their policy or policies in the usual form of such policy or policies, or in such other form and subject to such conditions as the said Lord High Treasurer or principal officer or officers of such office or department in which the said person or persons shall be appointed to such office or employment shall require, approve, and direct ; and the same, when taken and accepted, shall be in lieu of the security required by the said recited Acts or any of them.

This was a very important public recognition of the uses of Fidelity Insurance.

It may be well to state in this connection that personal interviews were had by the founders of the Guarantee Society with the then Chancellor of the Exchequer, the Right Hon. Henry Goulburn, as also with the preceding Chancellor, the Right Hon. F. T. Baring, at which the principles on which the business was founded were fully discussed ; and upon this the preceding measure was approved.

The union of Life Insurance with Fidelity Insurance was suggested in the following manner : The *British Surety* Company, projected in 1842 (while not itself intending to transact life business), proposed granting Fidelity policies on more favourable terms to persons whose lives were insured, " with the view and hope of inducing parties to cultivate a habit of economy, and lay the foundation for a future provision." Hence the applicants for insurance were to be divided into two classes :—1. Those who contracted simply for a guarantee for their fidelity ; they were charged according to a scale of premiums varying in ordinary cases from 10s. to 30s. per cent. 2. Those who contracted for a guarantee and were in possession of or effected a life policy ; for such persons the scale varied from 15s. to 40s., of which one-half was to be applied for the surety, and the remaining half to be expended in premiums on a policy for a principal sum payable at death, or at a certain age, or a deferred annual, at the option of the party insuring. The scheme did not mature.

1843.—Mr. Charles Saunderson, " late an auditor of the *Guarantee* Society " (and for some years afterwards deputy-chairman of the Society), published a pamphlet, " Suretiship. The Dangers and Defects of Private Security and their Remedy." The writer, referring to the then practice of the association, says :—

" Upon the appointment of an individual to any office or duty involving pecuniary trust, or upon the death of a surety, provided the applicant be found a person of moral worth, the Society are willing to incur the risk of becoming his bondsmen : the individual contributing to the funds of the Society a small percentage proportionate to the amount proposed to be named in the surety bond. *This percentage, however, is not calculated upon the degree of honesty he may be supposed to possess : if his reputation for strict integrity and morality present any blemish, he is rejected altogether.* Independently of the personal character of the individual, the Society is also guided by the nature of the engagement and the description of employment or business in which the bond or suretiship is required —the character of the referees and their connection with the party—the check under which the person will be placed for whom the security is sought, and the evidence the Society may obtain

that his conduct under these frequent and periodical checks will be observed by a wise and vigilant superior, and not abandoned to the common influences by which he may be surrounded. If the employer be careless or negligent, if he be generally known to be a person who does not exercise due caution in the protection of his own interests, by a strict supervision of the persons he employs, the Society declines to afford protection against the consequences to be expected from the defective arrangements of such an establishment ; so that the character of the individual seeking guarantee is but one of many circumstances which would affect its decision.

" A second main principle adopted is to treat losses by suretiship as an ordinary risk, and to protect the funds of the Society upon the general principles applicable to insurance, which are too well known to require a minute description : in all cases the individual who wishes to protect himself or others from any particular risk for which insurance exists pays a contribution into a general fund, smaller or greater in amount as the danger of loss increases or diminishes : and upon the occurrence of the casualty against which he provides, reimbursement is made from the general fund thus created."

He proceeds to say that there is much in the proceedings of such a society which tends to diminish the risk of suretiship to all concerned— which view we entirely endorse. He states his propositions hereon as follows :

" In the discharge of trusts between parties united by daily friendly intercourse, there is a natural repugnance to allude to a deed providing security for their faithful performance, and proceeding on the assumption of the possibility of dishonesty in a friend, in whatever station of life he may be placed. The instrument therefore loses much of its controlling power and is less likely to prevent fraud, than if the existence of the bond was periodically impressed upon the minds of all parties.

" The annual notice which the Society issues to the parties guaranted and to their principal, supplies this defect ; it reminds the one that holding the security of a bond, it is his duty to examine and balance periodically the accounts of the party guaranteed ; and to the other, it recalls every year the remembrance of the obligation under which he is bound to a faithful discharge of the trust he has undertaken to perform. It imposes no burthen upon the principal, unless an ordinary attention to his own interests can be so regarded ; and it requires from the servant nothing more than strict integrity of conduct. Not only therefore is a more complete security provided for the principal, but the Society encourages the growth of a high moral feeling in one of the most useful classes of the community—those entrusted with pecuniary transactions on account of others ; and watches with vigilance any sign of the deficiency of such principles, or the existence of pernicious habits. So convinced have many principals of well-established firms become of the great practical value of the position taken by the

Guarantee Society that they pay as a voluntary gift to the individual the amount of premium required by the Society from the person who is the subject of the guarantee."

The pamphlet then proceeds to point out several classes of occupations and employments in which the risk of Fidelity Insurance is great. It sums up generally under this head: "There are various other trades and professions that abound with temptation; and although the persons engaged therein receive very handsome pay and allowances, it has been found that in these trades the losses from dishonesty and fraud are proportionately high." It points to one advantage arising in actual experience. A firm charged one of its travellers with deficiency in his accounts. The Society insisted upon an examination of the accounts by way of proof. It turned out that there was no deficiency; but that on the contrary a sum was due from the firm to the traveller for services rendered.

The business in many of its details has been altered since this date; but its essential features remain the same. The conditions and stipulations of Fidelity policies will be stated at the close of the present article.—*Insurance Cyclopædia.*

(*To be continued.*)

THE ROYAL.

THE annual meetings and reports of even our most successful insurance companies seldom present any remarkable feature of novelty. They keep the even tenor of their way, and unless some extraordinary calamity, like the destruction of a great city by fire, has been encountered, the perusal of these yearly statements, however satisfactory to the business mind, is as monotonous as an oft-told tale. The annual report of the *Royal* Insurance Company, made on the 1st inst. at the shareholders' annual meeting in Liverpool, is, however, not only very pleasant reading to all pecuniarily interested in its prosperity, but also presents a surprise even for fire underwriters of the widest and longest experience.

Extraordinary success and extraordinary caution are seldom contemporaneous features in the same company, yet we find them co-existent in the *Royal*, as its last annual report shows. From this report we learn that the Company's fire premiums for 1883 were 4,913,685 dols., an increase over 1882 of 192,360 dols.; that the losses for the same period were 3,017,160 dols., being 65,060 dols. less than they were in 1882. Results so entirely gratifying, achieved in a season of adversity in which heavy disasters crowded constantly one upon another, would, it is natural to suppose, tempt the management to discard the idea of additional precaution, and indulge the shareholders in an exceedingly liberal division of profits. With a paid-up capital of 1,447,725 dols., a reserve fund of 4,750,000 dols., a fire fund of 2,750,000 dols., a profit and loss balance of 1,202,700 dols,, against a premium revenue of 4,913,685 dols., with its proportion of unexpired risks, the *Royal* appeared even to the most

provident and solicitous amply fortified at every point against all probable, if not all possible, contingencies. What more could be required to "make assurance double sure?"

The managers of the *Royal* have answered this question to their satisfaction by appropriating the increase of assets, derived from the enhanced value of the Company's investments, to the creation of a new account called the Conflagration Fund, amounting to 1,000,000 dols., to be added to the already abundant reserves of the *Royal*.

This lavish provision against extraordinary contingencies, such as the conflagration of large cities, which the experience of great agency fire insurance companies has taught them to anticipate, is altogether prudent and praiseworthy, not only as an efficient safeguard, but as a reliable guarantee that the confidence reposed in the management of the *Royal* and in its long-established reputation shall never be shaken by the heaviest loss that can befall the Company.

This pre-eminent position of strength and stability, reached long ago and held ever since by the *Royal*, enables it to pass through the worst years for fire underwriting without suffering any diminution of prestige or of ability to satisfy the reasonable dividend-cravings of its shareholders. The immense wealth and business momentum it has gained render any temporary inequality in its career almost imperceptible. Its good years, improved by the unrivalled harvesting skill and enterprise of its management, so far outnumber the bad, that the latter are but as ripples on the full and flowing stream of the Company's prosperity.

The *Royal's* territory is a vast one, taxing the ability of its officers and agents to the utmost, nowhere more than in the United States, which, as all underwriters can testify, has of late been most unpropitious for fire underwriting; yet the profits of the American branch for the six months ending June 30th, 1884, amounted to 85,068·49 dols., which was a triumph over difficulties overwhelming many that reflects great credit on the management of the agency. Last year the interest received on the investments of the *Royal* for its fire business was equal to 31 per cent. on its paid-up capital—1,447,725 dols., and yet the managers were not tempted to exceed the ordinary dividend, although some shareholders could not help feeling that the circumstances warranted the payment of a larger one than usual. The exercise of so much prudence and forbearance, coupled with masterly skill and consummate sagacity in underwriting, reveals the true secret of the *Royal's* splendid and constant success, world-wide popularity, and steady and massive growth.—*Insurance Times*, New York.

THE new law as proposed in Turkey will necessitate the insurance officers studying up the Koran, as all Turkish Law is based upon what is found in that book, and the proposed law makes Turkish justice final in all cases. "When in Turkey, do as the turkeys do," is the motto to be followed.

NOT ONE!

OUT of a thousand buildings, more or less durably constructed, how many will probably escape destruction by fire? Nine hundred and fifty, eh!

Out of a thousand men of strong and healthy constitutions, how many will escape death?

NOT ONE.

And yet you insure your house, but do not protect your life, as much more exposed as the proportion of two per cent. is greater than one-fourth of one per cent.

Captain Shaw, in his book on fire departments and the management of fires, severely criticises the American steam fire engine. He says:—The Americans long ago took the lead in steam fire engines, but they stopped where they began, and at this moment nearly all their splendid machines are far too heavy and unwieldy for the work, and the same may be said of almost everything they have in use. So heavy have their hose and other appliances become that they cannot be carried on the engines, and consequently every station has extra horses and coachmen at, of course, a considerable extra cost; but this is not the only drawback. The use of heavy appliances necessarily makes quick movements, even on the ground, most difficult, and on ladders, walls, or other heights, simply impossible. Moreover, in America the men are wrapped in heavy oilskins and sou'-westers, which retard their action and prevent them from getting close to their work. All over the continent of Europe, on the contrary, every effort has been made to lighten the appliances until, in the eyes of Americans, and sometimes even of Englishmen, they appear almost ridiculously small. Here in England, and notably in the capital, no effort has been spared to get all the appliances of the strongest and best kind for the hard, rough work, and, at the same time, of the greatest lightness consistent with the necessary strength; and the result is a sort of medium between the cumbrous and unwieldy materials used in America and the almost toy-like small gear on the continent of Europe. Many of the American steam engines are perfect models in every other point but fitness for the special work and lightness. In design, material, and workmanship, they compare favourably with any machinery ever made.

A close figurer writes: I have just increased my insurance to £10,000. I have intended to do this for a long time, but kept putting it off because I imagined I could not take the time to attend to it, but when the turning of my birthday approached, that is, six months after my birthday, when I found that by putting it off another day I would be rated at my age next birthday. On a policy of £4,000 the difference of one year in the age made a material increase in the cost of the insurance, not only for one year, but for every year as long as I live. It was too important a matter to ignore, therefore I took out my insurance at once and got it at the rate at my last birthday.

VALUATION RETURNS.

ALLIANCE.—Valuation Report for five years ending 31st December, 1883, on the Institute of Actuaries' table of mortality, 3 per cent. interest, and net premiums, shows a surplus of £140,560, of which £112,000 was divided among the policy-holders according to the following table:—

Years in force.	Age at Entry.			
	20	30	40	50
	£ s. d.	£ s. d.	£ s. d.	£ s. d.
5	8 0 2	9 3 1	10 14 0	12 14 1
10	7 8 0	8 9 0	9 16 4	11 18 8
15	6 17 6	7 18 2	8 19 5	11 13 9
20	6 6 11	7 5 2	8 8 7	11 3 7
25	5 18 10	6 12 8	8 5 1	11 12 7
30	5 9 0	6 4 7	7 17 11	12 12 8

The assurances in force amounted to £4,077,334. The life funds at same date, £1,288,647, or £31 12s. in hand against each £100 assured.—*Bourne's Handy Assurance Guide.*

Here is a strange incident, told in a telegram from Charlotte, N. C., under date of the 15th inst.: "Dr. Robert M. Williamson died to-day from the effects of fluid extract of aconite, which, it is said, he had taken to cause a reduction of his pulse-beat in order to obtain an insurance policy on his life." Well, he did reduce it.—*Insurance*, New York.

CPSIA information can be obtained
at www.ICGtesting.com
Printed in the USA
BVOW04s1049110917

494541BV00012B/203/P